Table of Contents

Table of Contents	1
KINGDOM SECRETS JESUS COULDN'T SHARE… UNTIL NOW!	4
About 'Kingdom Secrets'	5
CHAPTER 1I THE VOW OF PROSPERITY!	7
The Vow of Poverty	7
The most misunderstood Scriptures in Christendom.	8
Wealth is a mindset-Poverty is a set mind	10
The Kingdom- Heavens best kept secret!	11
CHAPTER 2I SEEK FIRST HIS KINGDOM & HIS RIGHTEOUSNESS!	13
Renewing our minds	13
All these THINGS will be added	15
What We Know about the Kingdom	17
1. The Kingdom + Righteousness unlocks material resources	19
2. The Kingdom is the most cryptic New Testament truth and equally the most misunderstood (It is only ever discussed by Jesus in parables).	19
3. Righteousness Positions you for Riches	20
4. Many Christians believe that by seeking a pure life devoted to God they are seeking Kingdom when they are still seeking righteousness.	21
Chapter 3I THE MASTER KEY PARABLE	22
Unlocking the Mystery	24
Why Parables?	26
Three Biblical Fruits	28
CHAPTER 4I TREASURE IN THE FIELD	29
Treasure Hunting	29
Seeking First the Kingdom	29
Why the Field and not the treasure?	30
Kingdom People pursue treasure righteously	30
Can our Dreams get in the way?	32
What is Treasure?	33
The Dream, The Domains, The Demands	34
1. Defining The Dream	36
2. Defining the Domain?	38
3. Defining the Demand	40
CHAPTER 5I THE TALENTS	43

Is Kingdom Economy Unfair?	43
Learning Outcomes?	50
Is God a Capitalist?	51
What We Can glean from this parable	52
CHAPTER 6I FIVE WISE THINGS TO LEARN FROM FIVE FOOLISH VIRGINS	59
The Parable of the virgins	59
Lesson 1I There are only two types of people in the Kingdom: Wise People and Foolish People	59
Lesson 2I You are only as wise as the five wisest people you choose to put in your life!	60
Lesson 3I Your friend Will determine your end.	63
Lesson 4I It is foolish to go through Life with a Lamp and nothing to Light it.	64
Lesson 5I Wise and Foolish People sleep two different types of sleep	65
CHAPTER 7I THE PRODIGAL SON	66
Why God isn't giving you the amount of money you asked Him for!	67
The winning lotto ticket ruined my life!	68
Is your desire to get rich as strong as your desire to get blessed?	71
CHAPTER 8I KOSMOS VERSUS KINGDOM	73
Why satan tried to kill Jesus, Judas and Job	73
Who is Satan?	76
The anointing Versus the glory	78
What is the job of the god of this world?	81
Where are you called to work?	87
CHAPTER 9I MONEY VERSUS MAMMON	88
Give to Caesar what belongs to Caesar!	88
Fiat Money & What Satan does not want you to know?	88
Why You can't serve both God and Mammon	89
Inflation Simplified	91
A Brief History of Fiat Currency	92
Rome	92
China	92
France	94
Germany	94
More Recent: Argentina, Mexico, Thai baht, Russia Zimbabwe	95
The Only way satan's system can work!	95
What is Money?	96
Money Belongs to God!	98

How Wealth Transfer will happen	99
CHAPTER 10l TAKING BACK WORLD KINGDOMS	101
Taking Back World Kingdoms	101
1. Know your Sphere of authority!	102
2. Know your End	104
3. Understand the 'whatever' anointing!	107

KINGDOM SECRETS JESUS COULDN'T SHARE... UNTIL NOW!

"I STILL HAVE MANY THINGS TO TELL YOU BUT YOU CAN'T HANDLE THEM NOW..."

This manuscript is protected under copyright law. It is strictly prohibited to duplicate the content of this manuscript for selling or sharing purposes without the written permission of the author. Any attempt to do so will be deemed a deliberate breach of this copyright agreement.

2016
All Rights Reserved

ISBN 978-0-244-67246-1

About 'Kingdom Secrets'

When I read John 16:12, I became increasingly intrigued not only by what the Bible says about Jesus and His Kingdom but what it does not say! At least not directly!

"I have much more to say to you, more than you can now bear.
But when he, the Spirit of truth, comes, he will guide you into all the truth. He will not speak on his own; he will speak only what he hears, and he will tell you what is yet to come.
John 16:12-13

Jesus admits deliberately omitting certain truths from the people of His age because it was "more than they could bear". What if The Holy Spirit over 2000 years later now wants to full disclosure so that you and I can prosper from truths that would have been unbearable before now?

As I looked deeper into my studies, I became increasingly aware that Jesus never omitted these truths at all, in fact He shared all of them. He immersed each of these blockbuster truths into children's stories. These children's fables were called parables! Parables comes from two words '*parallel*' and '*fables*'. Jesus used children's fables to covertly conceal and parallel ideals, policies and principles of His Kingdom. These truths went completely unnoticed by religious people and could somehow bypass their hearing ears.

He told them, "The secret of the kingdom of God has been given to you. But to those on the outside everything is said in parables so that, "'they may be ever seeing but never perceiving, and ever hearing but never understanding; otherwise they might turn and be forgiven!'
Mark 14:12-13

They are called the secrets of the Kingdom of God! When we understand these secrets there will be a release of transformation over Christendom that will cause us to operate in ways that religion previously did not give us permission to do. We will have a new referee and it will not be the law but grace!

This book will challenge your theology and cause a mind transformation that will ultimately challenge what you thought you knew about the Kingdom of God and His parables. It will show you practical ways to walk in Kingdom realities that will not only shape your spirituality but even transform the way you think about three of your greatest commodities: your time, your money and your friends!

When I was 23 years old, the Lord told me that he would interpret the parables of the kingdom of heaven to me and that it would release an end time season of financial privilege upon the body of Christ. I did not know that I would be a first fruit of this financial blessing, nor was I aware of the true meaning of persecution till the Lord started to bless me financially.

The moment the Lord unlocked 'Kingdom Secrets' to me, secrets that I now feel liberty to share with the body of Christ, I started a company that would grow to 5000 distributors and generate every month from its first month of operation around £12,000. My company was set to grow rapidly from its £144,000 a year foundation to reach an estimated £3million a year within two years. What excited me the most about this was I had no business acumen whatsoever. I was through and through a sold out preacher, living on shoe string budget at the time. I would accept speaking engagements that would generate a yearly income of around £1000 a year and that was only if the church was feeling generous at the time. Money and ministry was and still is a very awkward subject, especially in the UK where the jury is by and large still out on honouring itinerate ministers monetarily.

Let me start by saying what 'Kingdom Secrets' is not. It is not a get rich quick scheme! No where in this book will you find a prescription to short cuts to prosperity. Kingdom Secrets is prophetic insight into God's plan to prosper the church. Anyone who picks up this book and reads it will immediately be caused to think of the prosperity message differently. it altered my whole world at the age of 23 and brought me unforetold blessing that I had never known before in my life. The biggest thing having a lot of money taught me was that it is very easy to be wealthy but very hard to sustain it! If this book teaches you how to get rich but now how to stay wealthy then either I haven't written it well enough or you're not reading it thoroughly enough.

It has been entrenched in the fabric of the body of Christ that poverty is somehow servitude to God and that materialism is to be avoided at all costs in the pursuit for the ethereal. Famous songs I grew up on such as,

'Silver and gold, silver and gold, I'd rather have Jesus than silver and gold!'

How true it is that those of us who love Jesus have already come to the realisation that He is more worthy than anything in this world. But what if! What if you could have Jesus & SILVER & GOLD!

One of scriptures wealthiest men, Solomon had this to say:

money answers everything.
Ecclesiastes 10:19 ESV

What if the church is supposed to be the answer but we are questioned because we don't have the money to back our mission? What if the parables are hidden messages from God for our profiting? Enjoy this prophetic take on finances that I guarantee you have never heard anywhere before!

CHAPTER 1| THE VOW OF PROSPERITY!

The Vow of Poverty

"...There are other forms of consecrated life in the Catholic Church for men and women. They make a public profession of the evangelical counsels of chastity, poverty, and obedience, confirmed by a vow or other sacred bond, regulated by canon law but live consecrated lives in the world (i.e. not as members of a religious institute). Such are the secular institutes, the hermits and the consecrated virgins (canon 604) These make a public profession of the evangelical counsels by a vow or other sacred bond...."[1]

- It is unknown to me where the poverty message seeped into christianity. To the agnostic world this view of the church is a well accepted one. So much so that anyone claiming to be a member of 'the clothe' who owns possessions beyond what can be purchased in a local charity shop is deemed as dubious to the world and sadly the church. If we are going to take a journey into the world of prosperity, it is necessary for you to renounce this vow by making a new declaration. A declaration of prosperity!

- Repeat after me!

I_____ (insert name) renounce all vows of poverty ever spoken either by myself or by someone else on my families behalf. I declare today that I am covenanting with what the Bible says about my finances. I connect my economy to heavens economy and I repent of every time I have read the Bible religiously and leaned on my own understanding concerning money. I declare boldly that I can have God and wealth and that the Lord rejoices in my prosperity. (Psalm 35:27[2]**)**

- Now that you have chosen to start on the right foundation. Let's begin to correct some of the wrong foundations.

- Some of the scriptures we will endeavour to look at today are some of the most misunderstood scriptures in the whole of Christendom.

---

[1] https://en.wikipedia.org/wiki/Religious_vows

[2] "Let the LORD be magnified, which hath pleasure in the prosperity of his servant." KJV

The most misunderstood Scriptures in Christendom.

Briefly describe what the following scriptures mean to you:

1. The Love of money is the root of all evil (1Timothy 6:10)

   _____
   _____
   _____
   _____

2. "No one can serve two masters. Either you will hate the one and love the other, or you will be devoted to the one and despise the other. You cannot serve both God and money." (Luke 16:13)

   _____
   _____
   _____
   _____

3. "Blessed are the poor in spirit, for theirs is the kingdom of heaven. (Matthew 5:3)

   _____
   _____
   _____
   _____

4. But seek first his kingdom and his righteousness, and all these things will be given to you as well. (Matthew 6:33)

   _____
   _____
   _____
   _____

5. It is easier for a camel to go through the eye of a needle than for someone who is rich to enter the kingdom of God." (Mark 10:25)

   _____
   _____
   _____
   _____

- It is far too easy to look at all these scriptures and dismiss wealth all together to follow a life that abstains from materialistic ideals but the Bible is very clear that when looking at scripture we do not lean on our own understanding but acknowledge the Lord for the directing of our paths.[3]

- During the course of this material, I am going to attempt to give you a prophetic/apostolic view of financial prosperity and its place in your Christian life. Why? Because the Apostolic and Prophetic ministry breath revelation into the written word of God and unlock mysteries hidden deep within the text that the Bible tells us clearly the eyes of religion cannot see.

"Yes," said Jesus, "what sorrow also awaits you experts in religious law! For you crush people with unbearable religious demands, and you never lift a finger to ease the burden. What sorrow awaits you! For you build monuments for the prophets your own ancestors killed long ago. But in fact, you stand as witnesses who agree with what your ancestors did. They killed the prophets, and you join in their crime by building the monuments! This is what God in his wisdom said about you: 'I will send prophets and apostles to them, but they will kill some and persecute the others.'
Luke 11:46-49 (NLT)

- When you view finance from an Apostolic perspective and not a religious one, you begin to think differently. It is this rewiring in your thinking process that causes wealth to be attracted to you. After all the only people that fall into wealth by accident are the ones that play the lottery. If you are going to be wealthy, you have to deliberately convince yourself that you as a child of Christ have a right to it. Not only do you have a right but God has made a promise to the 'father of our faith'- Abraham to give the power to get wealth to anyone who claims to be his descendent.

You shall remember the LORD your God, for it is he who gives you power to get wealth, that he may confirm his covenant that he swore to your fathers, as it is this day.
Deuteronomy 8:18 (ESV)

- In fact, it is the very reason Christ redeemed us. So that we who are gentiles (non Jewish) can claim this same right to everything Abraham had.

He redeemed us in order that the blessing given to Abraham might come to the Gentiles through Christ Jesus.
Galatians 3:14 (NIV)

- Which Blessings? The ones written about in Genesis 12. Find below a list of them:
  1. I will make your family great
  2. I will bless you
  3. I will make you famous
  4. You will be a blessing
  5. I will bless people who bless you
  6. I will curse people who curse you
  7. People you come in contact with will be blessed because you are there.

---
[3] Proverbs 3:5-6

- This is God's promise and Jesus died not just to redeem you but to restore all the promises of Abraham on to you.

- The work of the cross was a finished work. Jesus doesn't redeem anything He doesn't plan to restore.

Wealth is a mindset-Poverty is a set mind

- You have picked up this manual because you want to be wealthy and it just so happens that we have written it because we want to show you exactly how. You see, wealth like poverty is a mentality we develop over time. In fact, as you will see through reading this manual that if your approach to wealth is passive as opposed to tactile then you will never receive what you do not intend on receiving and you will never get what you do not make room for.

- The only poor people in life are adults. Children are always rich! Which is why they always expect food to be on the table, school fees to be paid etc .The older we become the more we pick up on a survivors mentality as opposed to the success we once had as children. If you are going to be wealthy then you must acquire a wealthy mentality.

- Notice, we said mentality and not mind otherwise you would think that we were telling you to go back to school and get an education. Some of the most educated people are poor because a rich mind without a rich mentality is just like a polystyrene cup with holes in it. It may be full of substance but it's always leaking.

- Whilst education is good, successful people don't always know what to do but they do what they know. This is the difference between being smart and being wise. It is better to know something and do something than to know everything and do nothing.

- You may not be the most educated person and you may be in a terrible financial situation where you feel like giving up on yourself but I want to show you the secret to amassing great levels of wealth without compromising your faith in Christ in the process.

- Wealth is nothing short of a mind set but poverty is nothing short of a set mind. If we are ever going to achieve wealth then we must change the way we see money. We must partner with the vow of prosperity that God made to Abraham. Insert your name here and recite this truth every day for the next 30 days before you go to bed and when you wake up in the morning.

    1. _____ God's promised He will make your family great!
    2. _____ God's promised He will bless you!
    3. _____ God's promised He will make you famous!
    4. _____ God's promised you will be a blessing!
    5. _____ God's promised He will bless people who bless you!
    6. _____ God's promised He will curse people who curse you!
    7. _____ God's promised that people you work with, live with and be with are blessed because of you.

- Keep saying it until you feel the scales of religiosity fall of you. Convince your fallen mind to accept the promises of a risen Christ. Once you do this, you will already begin to experience a worth transfer that will set in motion a wealth transfer.

For as he thinks within himself, so he is
Proverbs 23:7 (NASB)

The Kingdom- Heavens best kept secret!

- Question: What is implicit in somebody giving you keys? Surely the presence of keys has to allude to the fact that 1. There is a door, 2. The door is shut, 3. The door is locked most likely because 4. there is something precious on the inside that must be kept safe.

- Jesus gave keys to Peter. These were not keys to a church but in actual fact they were called 'Keys to the kingdom of heaven'.[4] This tells me 1. The kingdom has a door. 2. The door is shut. 3. The door is locked most likely because 4. There is something precious on the other side that must be kept safe.

- Why would Jesus give Peter an open church but keys to a locked kingdom. Because Peter represents an Apostolic/Prophetic breed that can understand the kingdom and reveal it to the church in such a way that they will be freed from religion to walk in righteousness and riches.

- The devil cannot afford for this breed to get out. I call them 'key keepers' because they have an ability to decipher the most mystifying details of the text in such a way that the church becomes liberated from legalism and materialistic guilt. So vehement is the devil that this breed does not get into the church that he confines them to church history, persecution or death should they ever choose to leave theology and actually emerge as mighty ones in the earth.

- This breed is alive and well today but hiding in caves in the crevices of Europe. Full of mystery and yet to the religious church their apostolic authority will be deemed as apostate audacity. Yet without them the Bible remains a legal book and not a living 'present truth revelation.

This is what God in his wisdom said about you: 'I will send prophets and apostles to them, but they will kill some and persecute the others.' "As a result, this generation will be held responsible for the murder of all God's prophets from the creation of the world— from the blood of Abel to the blood of Zechariah, who was killed between the altar and the sanctuary. Yes, I tell you, this generation will be held responsible for it all. "What sorrow awaits you experts in religious law! For you remove "*The key to knowledge*" from the people. You don't enter the Kingdom yourselves, and you prevent others from entering."
Luke 11:49-52 (NLT)

- These Apostles and Prophets carry the **key of knowledge**. The Bible is knowledge concealed but the prophets and apostles give the church knowledge revealed. As a new breed of this apostolic/prophetic movement, you are the apostate of your world.

---

[4] I will give you the keys of the kingdom of heaven; whatever you bind on earth will be bound in heaven, and whatever you loose on earth will be loosed in heaven." Matthew 16:19 (NIV)

Every apostolic/prophetic movement started as an apostate movement. Jesus said that if they call Him satan how much more his students.[5]

- John was an called an apostate because he didn't eat or drink like everybody else. Jesus was called an apostate because he ate, drank, made merry with tax collectors and healed on the Sabbath day, Paul was called apostate because he preached the gospel of Jews to gentiles (outsiders) baptising them in the name of Jesus. Apostles of tomorrow were apostates of today!

- Why? Because they have a key that doesn't stray from the scripture but can unlock it in such a tangible and fruitful way.

- I believe that this next move of the Spirit of God is going to be given to a church that understands the mystery of the kingdom. Notice I said mystery. Every parable Jesus taught was on the kingdom. He was waiting for apostolic/prophetic unlocking at a time the church could bear it.

- We are going to see a breed of righteous and rich saints in the church again. This breed will be seen as apostates and deserters of the faith because they have fame, favour and the confidence to use their wealth to influence policies, shift culture and change laws.

- In chapter two we will look at what Jesus meant by "Seek first the Kingdom of heaven and His righteousness and all these things will be added.

---

[5] Matthew 10:25 "It is enough for students to be like their teachers, and servants like their masters. If the head of the house has been called Beelzebub, how much more the members of his household!" (NIV)

CHAPTER 21 SEEK FIRST HIS KINGDOM & HIS RIGHTEOUSNESS!

Renewing our minds

- Let us now take a look at one of our most misunderstood texts in the Bible. In it Jesus instructs us to seek first His kingdom

But seek first his kingdom and his righteousness, and all these things will be given to you as well.
Matthew 6:33 NIV

- Understanding this scripture will be key to unlocking an understanding in the whole of the New Testament that until now the Bible tells us has been hidden.
- In fact you have an excuse not to fully understand what Jesus was truly talking about in this scripture because His own disciples seemed just as mystified as to Jesus' attempts to make the revelation of the Kingdom of God in as cryptic a way as possible.

The disciples came to him and asked, "Why do you speak to the people in parables?"
Matthew 10:13 (NIV)

- In order to fully understand what Jesus was talking about in Matthew 6:33 we have to retrace our steps and look at the whole of Chapter 6. Understanding it will be the difference between living a Christian life of poverty or wealth.

- This scripture alone has led to the justification of those who believe that Christians are not entitled to anything of materialistic value. So let's take a look at it again with fresh eyes.

    (You may want to pray with your students at this point- That God would give all of you revelation in the knowledge of Him. Take your time looking through chapter 6 and ask yourselves the following questions.)

1. What three things is this chapter telling us to do in our practice of righteousness?

2. Is giving an act of practicing righteousness?

3. Does Christ saying 'When you give' signify an assumption that you are in a place to be a resource to the needy?

4. Is there some kind of currency I receive from God for practicing righteousness in secret? If so… what is it? See Matt 6:4, 6:6, 6:18

5. Does Christ saying I can't serve both God and money signify that I have to make a choice which one I am going to have in my life or does it speak to priority? See Matt 6:24

6. Is Christ against savings when he says- *"Do not store up for yourselves treasures on earth, where moths and vermin destroy, and where thieves break in and steal."* (Matt 6:19) If not, what is he asking me to do here and how can I practically do it?

7. In Matthew 6:25, is Christ teaching us to against materialism?

_____
_____
_____
_____

8. If Christ is telling me to seek His Kingdom and His Righteousness what does it mean to seek His Kingdom?

_____
_____
_____
_____

All these THINGS will be added

- The entirety of Matthew 6 speaks of the practice of righteousness as three forms starting with
  1. Giving,
  2. Praying,
  3. Fasting

"So when you give…"
Matthew 6:2

"And when you pray…"
Matthew 6:5

"When you fast"
Matthew 6:16

- If the scripture in Matthew 6:33 could be understood from excluding the kingdom i.e.

  seek ye first the righteousness of God and all these things would be added
  Matthew 6:33 (edited)

- If this was all Jesus was asking us as Christians to do, many of us wouldn't have a problem because they are things we ought to be doing as believers.
-
- 'When' as a prefix indicates that the Lord already assumes this is a part of your practice as a Christian believer: That you are giving, praying and fasting

- It also speaks about God giving a renumeration for your practice of these three facets of righteousness in secret.

- In this scripture however, we understand that by seeking the kingdom and righteousness we get access to these things! What things? Matthew 6:25 tells us what they are!

    1. Food
    2. Drink
    3. Clothes
    4. Your Life
    5. Your Body
    6. Todays provision

- Is it possible that we have ignored a God who wants to give us 'THINGS?'
-
- Christ here in this scripture is trying to give us a blue print to access material things. If He wasn't He would not have said *"all these things will be added to you"* in your pursuit of seeking His Kingdom and His righteousness.
-
- Most people when it comes to getting things from the Lord pray more, fast more and may even give more failing to understand that doing these things in secret will unlock a spiritual reward but not necessarily a material one.
-
- Material rewards come when we combine a righteous life with a kingdom life.

His divine power has granted to us all things that pertain to life and godliness, through the knowledge of him who called us to his own glory and excellence
2 Peter 1:3 (ESV)

- Righteousness reaps godly rewards, but kingdom pursuit reaps reward both in heaven and in this lifetime.

"Yes," Jesus replied, "and I assure you that everyone who has given up house or wife or brothers or parents or children, for the sake of the Kingdom of God, will be repaid many times over in this life, and will have eternal life in the world to come."
Luke 8:29-30 (NLT)

- It should be clear that seeking righteousness guarantees earthly rewards but that God has planned earthly rewards for those who seek His kingdom and His righteousness. Although we are clear on what His righteousness is, the Bible is somewhat cryptic on what His kingdom is.

- It is far too easy to gloss over this scripture and believe that if we just keep seeking God that we are somehow seeking His Kingdom. If it were that easy we would all be very well off by now. Rather we have to get used to a God whose very godliness is tied to the secrets He keeps and the ones He chooses to share.

It is the glory of God to conceal a matter; to search out a matter is the glory of kings.
Proverbs 25:2 (NIV)

What We Know about the Kingdom

Here's what we know about the Kingdom. (We will attempt to explain these things in our groups as we go along but for now it's important just to know the points.)

1. The Kingdom + Righteousness unlocks material resources. Whereas righteousness minus the kingdom stores up future ethereal resources.

2. The Kingdom is the most cryptic New Testament truth and equally the most misunderstood (It is only ever discussed by Jesus in parables).

3. It is impossible to be righteous without being born again but it is possible to be kingdom without being righteous.

4. Many people think they are seeking the kingdom but are actually seeking righteousness and are storing eternal wealth as opposed to unlocking present wealth.

5. God's church is open God's Kingdom is locked. God's church is about attendance, God's kingdom is about attention.

6. The kingdom is not in the church- the church is in the Kingdom.

7. The parables Jesus taught on the kingdom all have to do with buying, selling, investing and money.

Explain your understanding of these terms taking notes as you go along! If you are unsure just try your best before you move on to research the following points to come to a conclusion. You can work in groups or on your own.

1. The Kingdom + Righteousness unlocks material resources

"Truly I tell you," Jesus said to them, "no one who has left home or wife or brothers or sisters or parents or children for the sake of the kingdom of God will fail to receive many times as much in this age, and in the age to come eternal life."
Luke 18:29-30 (NIV)

- Jesus tells the disciples who have left everything for the sake of the kingdom of God that they will receive it back in their lifetime.

- The message version of this text says whatever you lose out will come back multiplied many times over in your lifetime.

"Yes," said Jesus, "and you won't regret it. No one who has sacrificed home, spouse, brothers and sisters, parents, children—whatever—will lose out. It will all come back multiplied many times over in your lifetime. And then the bonus of eternal life!"
Luke 18:29-30 (The Message)

- God clearly has a plan for your finances to be unlocked by your ability to seek His kingdom and His righteousness.

- In Matthew 6:33 He says that He will give you all these things: Including food, drink, clothes and what you need for your life, your body and your tomorrow. He will take care of it in His kingdom package.

- Whilst we all know what it means to follow righteousness, we will begin to take a look at what it truly means to follow the kingdom and separate yourself from a kosmos culture in the next chapter titled- Kingdom versus Kosmos.

- Many christians do not realise that they are still kosmos kids and not kingdom kids. We will look at the differences more in the next chapter but for now be assured that God wants to give you things!

But seek first his kingdom and his righteousness, and all these things will be given to you as well.
Matthew 6:33 NIV

2. The Kingdom is the most cryptic New Testament truth and equally the most misunderstood (It is only ever discussed by Jesus in parables).

- Jesus never told us what the kingdom was. Although in Matthew 6 He spends time detailing what righteousness is, he never actually once says the kingdom of heaven is.

- Even Apostle Paul never told us what the Kingdom of heaven was, rather the vital components that go into our understanding of the Kingdom of God saying…

**For the kingdom of God is not a matter of eating and drinking, but
of righteousness, peace and joy in the Holy Spirit
Romans 14:17 (NIV)**

- Although Jesus taught often about the kingdom of God, He never once says what it is but He does say what it is like.

**"For the kingdom of heaven is like a landowner who went out early
in the morning to hire workers for his vineyard.
Matthew 20:1 (NIV)**

**"The kingdom of heaven is like a mustard
seed, which a man took and planted in his field
Matthew 13:31**

**the kingdom of heaven is like a net that was let
down into the lake and caught all kinds of fish
Matthew 13:47 (NIV)**

- So cryptic was the message of the Kingdom that the disciples in Matthew 13:10 asked Jesus why He spoke in this cryptic language called parables when it came to understanding the Kingdom. Jesus responded!

**This is why I speak to them in parables: "Though seeing, they do not see; though hearing, they do not hear or understand. In them is fulfilled the prophecy of Isaiah: "'You will be ever hearing but never understanding; you will be ever seeing but never perceiving.
Matthew 13:13-14 (NIV)**

---

3. Righteousness Positions you for Riches

* If God levied our income on the basis of our righteousness, it would most likely fluctuate depending on our temperament.

* Such a system of riches for righteousness would violate the law of grace which is unmerited favour.

* If God were to merit us on the basis of how good we were then there would be no need for Jesus. We would simply have a Santa Claus system- where if you are good you get gifts and if you are bad you get none.

* Righteousness does not entitle you to riches, righteousness positions you for riches.

**A good person leaves an inheritance for their children's children, but a sinner's wealth is stored up for the righteous.
Proverbs 13:22 (NIV)**

**what he lays up the righteous will wear, and the innocent will divide his silver.
Job 27:17 (NIV)**

---

4. Many Christians believe that by seeking a pure life devoted to God they are seeking Kingdom when they are still seeking righteousness.

- Christ is our righteousness but Jesus clearly points out that righteousness practices in three ways. 1. How you give, 2. How you pray and 3. How you fast.

- Righteousness reaps heavenly reward but as we have seen in Matthew 6- Kingdom releases 'things' that you need here and right now.

- For far too long the church has assumed that by seeking righteousness God will take care of their riches.

- Whilst it is true that righteousness positions you to be rich, your store of righteousness can only be deposited into your earthly life by an in-depth understanding of Kingdom principles as we will see in the next Session.

- In the next session we will begin to look at the parables. Unlocking each one for its powerful mysteries.

Chapter 3| THE MASTER KEY PARABLE

- We will begin with what the master key parable. We call it the master key parable because Jesus said of this parable in Mark that if you do not understand this parable then you will not understand all of the parables.

Then Jesus said to them, "If you can't understand the meaning of this parable, how will you understand all the other parables?
Mark 4:13 (NLT)

- Our understanding of this parable begins with erasing any preconceived notions when it comes to it. Let's take a look at the same parable in Matthew 13:4

And he spake many things unto them in parables, saying, Behold, a sower went forth to sow; And when he sowed, some *seeds* fell by the way side, and the fowls came and devoured them up: Some fell upon stony places, where they had not much earth: and forthwith they sprung up, because they had no deepness of earth: And when the sun was up, they were scorched; and because they had no root, they withered away. And some fell among thorns; and the thorns sprung up, and choked them: But other fell into good ground, and brought forth fruit, some an hundredfold, some sixtyfold, some thirtyfold. Who hath ears to hear, let him hear.
Matthew 13:3-9 (KJV)

- In groups of two or on your own attempt to answer the following questions without looking at the answers. It will help deal with any preconceived notions surrounding this parable to write them out in chronology.

1. What is this parable in general talking about?
___
___
___
___

2. Who is the sower?
___
___
___
___

3. What is the seed?
___
___
___
___

4. Who is the wayside?

5. Who are the fowls?

6. What are the stony places?

7. What are the thorns?

8. What do you consider to be good ground?

9. What does the Bible mean by bringing forth fruit of 30, 60 and a hundred fold?

Unlocking the Mystery

- Matthew 13:3-9 begs the question, what type of Christian are you.

- It breaks down the believer into three basic archetypes. Wayside, stony, thorny good.

- Let's now begin to answer the previous questions one by one.

1. What is this parable in general talking about?

Jesus tells us in the same chapter what this parable is speaking about. He says it is about the message of the Kingdom and four types of hearers:

**When any one heareth the word of the kingdom
Matthew 13:19 (KJV)**

**a. Heard but did not understand- Path
b. Understood but did not stand- Stony
c. Understood but did not withstand- Thorny
d. Understood- Good**

2. Who is the sower?

The Sower in this case is God.

3. What is the seed?

The seed is the word of the kingdom. It is a seed because it has not yet germinated. It is concealed. Many have interpreted it as the word of the gospel and the soils to four different types of hearts. Jesus tells us in this chapter that the seed is the word of the Kingdom not the message of the gospel.

**WHEN ANY ONE HEARETH THE WORD OF THE KINGDOM...
MATTHEW 13:19 (KJV)**

4. Who is wayside? (heard but did not understand)

Wayside is anyone on the path who hears the word of the kingdom and simply does not understand it. Notice, in this scripture Jesus never once alluded to disbelief but misunderstanding. This soil is not to be mistaken for an unbeliever who does not receive Christ. But rather a hearer who does not understand kingdom. This parable does not talk about the unbelieving hearer but the believing but not understanding hearer.

5. Who are the fouls?

The fouls speaks of the wicked one known as satan. The Bible says he *harpazó* what was sown in the heart. This word means to catch away as if by stealing. The devil is a thief and thieves only rob precious things. This same word is used in

describing the kingdom and the fact that violent men have been robbing it in Matthew 11:12. (which we will talk about later)

6. What are the stony places? (understand but did not stand)

The stony ground defines the hearers that understand but do not make a stand. They have no root (revelation) in themselves. These have not owned the revelation of the kingdom but have borrowed their understanding of it from an explanation. They spring up and are excited and look as if they are about to bear fruit but trouble or persecution comes because of the word of the kingdom so they fall away quickly.

During this course, you will have the opportunity to be rooted in a revelation that will quite possibly alter your financial landscape forever. You will have a choice to be rooted or excited. People who do not experience fruit from this teaching need only ask if they have any root in this teaching. Firmly root yourself in the kingdom principles to avoid being stony.

7. What are the thorns? (understand but did not withstand)

The thorns are those consumed with the cares of life and the deceitfulness of wealth. This type is arguably one step away from being fruitful hearers but they are so entrenched in a systemic form of thinking that they are choked up from producing fruit. They live on a worry based economy and are content with fiscal control and reward systems that involve little to no risk.

To avoid being in this place does not mean avoiding life or wealth but it does mean avoiding the cares of life and the deceitfulness of wealth which is:

1. **Worry, doubt and fear.**
2. **Lust of the eyes, Lust of the Flesh and Pride of Life.**

It means leaving a fear based economy (we will discuss this later).

8. What is good ground?

Good ground according to Matthew 13:23 refers to "someone who hears the word and understands it!" This Word is not understanding an understanding of the gospel but an understanding of the kingdom. Jesus said not everyone with ears to hear will truly understand but this soil hears it and just gets it. Their understanding is proven in the fruit they bring forth.

9. What does the Bible mean by bringing forth fruit of 30, 60 and a hundred fold?

It is far too easy to assume this fruit is somehow
1. Fruit of the spirit- Fruit of the spirit in Galatians is singular and has many facets including love, joy, peace patience...
2. It is far too easy to assume it is a harvest of souls. Although this can equally be taken from this parables prophetic meaning.
3. This parable refers to fruit in folds. Stating that some receive

- 100 times as much from their understanding!
- 60 times as much from their understanding!

- **Some 30 times as much from their understanding!**

This understanding of folds speak about the gains of farming which symbolically can refer to the winning of souls by virtue of understanding kingdom mystery but also the gaining of resource or profit from understanding kingdom mysteries.

Which Soil Best describes you (Give yourself an honest evaluation)

a. I hear it but I don't understand it- Wayside ☐

b. I understand it and it excites me but I don't want others to think I'm all about money- Stony ☐

c. I understand it but I fear what leaving my economy to follow God's might do- Thorny ☐

d. I Understand that wealth is a part of God's Kingdom strategy and that I grow in financial integrity- Good ☐

Why Parables?

The disciples came to him and asked, "Why do you speak to the people in parables?" He replied, "Because the knowledge of the secrets of the kingdom of heaven has been given to you, but not to them. Whoever has will be given more, and they will have an abundance. Whoever does not have, even what they have will be taken from them.
Matthew 13:11-12 (NIV)

- Jesus speaks in parables because He only wants the knowledge of the secrets of His Kingdom to be kept in righteous hands.

- To truly enter the kingdom of God one must be born again but to experience the Kingdom of God you simply have to have understanding.

- The disciples at this point were not born again but yet they could experience kingdom by just having ears to hear and eyes to see what the Spirit was saying.

- It is possible to be a Christian outside of the kingdom and it is equally possible to be a non Christian inside the kingdom.

"THEREFORE I TELL YOU THAT THE KINGDOM OF GOD WILL BE TAKEN AWAY FROM YOU AND GIVEN TO A PEOPLE WHO WILL PRODUCE ITS FRUIT.
MATTHEW 12:43 (NIV)

- The kingdom was meant for the church but if the church does not produce the fruit of the kingdom then it will be given to a people producing its fruit.

- Remember this word *Harpazó*. It referred to the foul of the air coming and stealing what was sown in the mans heart who fell on the wayside soil.

- Many Christians fail to realise that although Jesus is THE Way, THE Truth and THE life that there is another way in to the Kingdom!

**"TRULY, TRULY, I SAY TO YOU, HE WHO DOES NOT ENTER THE SHEEPFOLD BY THE DOOR BUT CLIMBS IN BY ANOTHER WAY, THAT MAN IS A THIEF AND A ROBBER.
JOHN 10:1 (NIV)**

- This is why the Bible says:

**FROM THE DAYS OF JOHN THE BAPTIST UNTIL NOW, THE KINGDOM OF HEAVEN HAS BEEN SUBJECTED TO VIOLENCE, AND VIOLENT PEOPLE HAVE BEEN RAIDING IT.
MATTHEW 11:12 (NIV)**

- Notice this scriptures reference to violent man *harpazó* which means to raid, steal or loot.

- Jesus desire is for the church to experience the fruit of the kingdom. In doing so He declares that if you want the Crown you have to take up the cross. In essence no righteousness no riches.

- Yet it seems that the world has found a way to access the crown without the cross and the church has formed a culture that denies themselves their kingdom inheritance.

- There are two people in the kingdom right now
  1. Those that are born in to it
  2. Those that break in to it

- Satan in Genesis knew that He had lost the way in to the Kingdom so he stole His way in from Adam.

- Yes Jesus is the Way but there is another way and Jesus does not want people to enter in without going through Him the gate!

- Parables are the strategy for protecting Kingdom truths and treasures. (We will see this as we look at the other parables)

- Jesus is not protecting these truths from the world nor is he preserving them for the church. He is preserving these truths for those who actually want to bring forth the fruit of a Kingdom lifestyle.

Three Biblical Fruits

- There are three types of fruit the Bible talks about!

1. The fruit of the spirit- Galatians 5:22- Fruit which the Holy Spirit produces in my born again spirit.

2. The fruit of righteousness- Philippians 1:11- The fruit which Jesus produces in my time spent with Him and His word. The evidence of which is prayer, fasting and giving in secret so as not to be self righteous.

3. The fruit of the kingdom- The fruit of prosperity made manifest in people and resources that come into my life to fulfil my God given assignment and to live a fulfilled life. (Matthew 13:8)

CHAPTER 4| TREASURE IN THE FIELD

Treasure Hunting

- This next parable Jesus speaks brings greater clarity to what the Kingdom of heaven is like.

Again, the kingdom of heaven is like unto treasure hid in a field; the which when a man hath found, he hideth, and for joy thereof goeth and selleth all that he hath, and buyeth that field.
Matthew 13:44 (KJV)

- Notice again the unique references to finances. Jesus is using the simile of treasure in a field to help bring to light a greater understanding of the Kingdom. As we shine light on this understanding there is one vital question you should already be asking yourself.

- Why did the man sell everything he had to purchase the field and not the treasure?

_____
_____
_____

Seeking First the Kingdom

- What if Matthew 6:33 can now be read in conjunction with Matthew 13:44. Would it slightly make more sense as to Jesus instructions when it came to provision.

- Let's remind ourselves that He said not to worry about clothes, food, drink, provision, tomorrow. Basically not to worry about materialistic things. Remember, He never said not to be materialistic but just not to worry about materials. Finishing His statement by assuring you "Your heavenly Father knows you have need of them...." (Matthew 6:32). He then offers a strategy for getting them

But seek first his kingdom and his righteousness, and all these things will be given to you as well.
Matthew 6:33 (NIV)

- What if we took this Matthew 13:44 parable and combined the two like a jigsaw piece. We already know that God wants us to have these things but not to have the same materialistic pursuit of them that the world has.

- What if we have mistaken the fruit of kingdom for the fruit of righteousness which He also adds as a conjunctive term to our pursuit of Kingdom. Let's see what it would read.

But seek first His treasure and His righteousness, and all these things will be given to you as well
Matthew 6:33 (NIV)

Why the Field and not the treasure?

* Whatever the field was in this case was not as relevant as the fact that there was treasure in it.

* The man purchased the field for three reasons:

  1. There was treasure in the field!
  2. The field is cheaper than the treasure
  3. Once he buys the field he automatically owns the treasure in the field.

- Notice this man hid the treasure. He was not willing that others should know the opportunity that He had stumbled into. This is not a gospel message! The gospel is not to be hidden but proclaimed. This is a kingdom revealed strategy!

- The word treasure is the greek word *thésauros* it means:
  1. A storehouse for precious things
  2. A repository
  3. Wealth
  4. A Coffer

- The kingdom of heaven is like wealth hidden in a field which when a man had found he hid and for joy sold all he had to purchase the field.

Kingdom People pursue treasure righteously

But seek first his kingdom and his righteousness, and all these things will be given to you as well.
Matthew 6:33 (NIV)

- Riches are for the righteous. Christ came to demonstrate this as the first fruit of a new breed of priesthood.

- Christ was not an Aaronite or Levitical Priest. Christ was after the order of a rare breed of Priesthood called the Melchizedek order.

And he says in another place, "You are a priest forever, in the order of Melchizedek."
Hebrews 5:6 (NIV)

- Had Jesus not been from this order- Matthew 6:33 would have been an illegal statement for Him to make. This is because Priests had not inheritance in business, land or material possessions. Their inheritance by law was the Lord.

The LORD said to Aaron, "You will have no inheritance in their land, nor will you have any share among them; I am your share and your inheritance among the Israelites.
Numbers 18:20 (NIV)

Therefore, Levi does not have a portion or inheritance with his brothers; the LORD is his inheritance, just as the LORD your God spoke to him.)
Deuteronomy 10:9 (NIV)

- Before Melchizedek the priests job was to pursue righteousness and to consecrate God's people. Melchizedek however represents a new breed of priesthood. A priesthood capable of being a priest and a king simultaneously.

This Melchizedek was king of Salem and priest of God Most High. He met Abraham returning from the defeat of the kings and blessed him, and Abraham gave him a tenth of everything. First, the name Melchizedek means "king of righteousness"; then also, "king of Salem" means "king of peace.
Hebrews 7:1-2 (NIV)

- Melchizedek was a king of peace and a priest of righteousness. He held dual offices!

- The word peace here is the greek word *eiréné*. It means:

1. Welfare- the state of doing well especially in respect to good fortune, happiness, well-being, or prosperity

2. Prosperity- the condition of being successful or thriving, the state of being successful usually by making a lot of money

Where our forerunner, Jesus, has entered on our behalf. He has become a high priest forever, in the order of Melchizedek.
Hebrews 6:20 (NIV)

- In Christ Jesus we too are after this order. This means we are entitled to an inheritance in the Lord and an inheritance in the land.

And hast made us unto our God kings and priests: and we shall reign on the earth.
Revelation 5:10 (KJV)

Can our Dreams get in the way?

Christianity is not about pursuing your dream, it is about pursuing God's dream and your part in it. - Author unknown

Is this a true statement? If so Why?

_____
_____
_____
_____

- For too long the church has been taught to chase the big dream and follow your destiny, knowing that God is with you. However, the Bible teaches us that so often one of eight things contradict God's purposes in our lives being fulfilled.

1. Our plan- Proverbs 19:21, Psalm 33:10, Proverbs 16:9
2. Our desires- Psalm 37:4, Psalm 145:19, Psalm 73:25
3. Our will- Luke 22:42
4. Our thoughts- Isaiah 55:8,
5. Our ways- Isaiah 55:8, Psalm 86:11, Psalm 37:5, Psalm 27:11, Exodus 33:13
6. Our heart- Jeremiah 17:9, Mark 7:21,
7. Our purpose- Isaiah 46:10
8. Other People- Psalm 146:3, Psalm 60:11, Isaiah 2:22, Jeremiah 17:5

- If we are asking God "What is your plan to make me wealthy?" We are asking the wrong question.

- If we are asking God "When can you give me money to serve you better?" We are still asking amiss.

- But if we are asking God, "What is your plan for money and my part in it" then we begin to start asking with some sense of clarity.

- There is no such thing as a perfect married couple but there is such a thing as a perfect marriage. The Bible lays out a system for imperfect people to perfect your marriage if only they abide by God's plan and purpose not for them but for marriage!

- God's plan, desire, will, thoughts, ways, heart and purpose is so much better and more immaculate in its conception than we even have a mind for.

- If we understand God's plan for money then we can begin to insert ourselves into that narrative.

- It is not about being thee player, just the participant. If your whole life and mindset about money is to be thee guy, and thee boss, and thee entrepreneur then your ambition may get you your wealth at the cost of your health and only to buy back your health at the cost of your wealth.

- Those who became wealthy in the Bible found a way to insert themselves into God's existing plan for money. Not their money, just money!

- If you understand that money has no bias, people can be racist, hateful, stingy but money can't be any of these things then you will spend less time exerting your strength and more time inserting yourself into the existing narrative of how God has always made money work.

- There are two types of people when it comes to making money:
  1. Those who work for money
  2. Those who have money work for them

- People who work for money use all their time to get money.

- People who have money work for them use all their money to get time.

- The difference here is a value system.

- What is your greatest commodity?
  1. Money?
  2. Time?

**Do not wear yourself out to get rich; do not trust your own cleverness.
Cast but a glance at riches, and they are gone, for they will surely sprout wings and fly off to the sky like an eagle.
Proverbs 23:4-5 (NIV)**

What is Treasure?

- The parable of the the different grounds teaches us the first thing we need to know about money. Receiving it is about understanding- nothing more, nothing less! Those who have it simply understand God's plan for it. Saved and unsaved! They know how to produce fruit from it 100, 60 and 30 times as much.

- The treasure in the field parable however teaches us the second vital truth about money. Wealth is more about treasure than it is about pleasure.

- God has wealth prepared in the earth for the righteous. This wealth is hidden for anyone who understands to grab a hold of. Notice, the parable doesn't say a Christian man found it but just a man found it. This scripture could have just as easily been a woman. But what is treasure?

- Treasure is a commodity- A commodity is something useful or valued.

- In essence a commodity is what people want, need and are willing to pay for.

- This man found something that others were willing to pay for so he hid it for joy.

- God does not give wealth! He simply gives the power to get wealth to anyone who is willing to understand how money works.

But remember the LORD your God, for it is he who gives you the ability to produce wealth, and so confirms his covenant, which he swore to your ancestors, as it is today.
Deuteronomy 8:18 (NIV)

- You cannot find treasure in the pursuit of pleasure!

- The difference between treasure and pleasure is pleasure is what you do that you want people to one day like but treasure is what you find that others already like.

- Pleasure is what you want to do, treasure is what other people want to do! When you find a way to align your pleasure with God's treasure then you have just crossed into the economic equaliser of a lifetime. So few people find this intersection in destiny!

- I call it the treasure/pleasure tipping point! It is the point at which a Christian believer stops asking God to fulfil their dreams but starts seeing life from God's dreams.

- God has already put in the earth everything the church will need to succeed. Every resource and supply but if the church becomes a ground to fulfil dreams and not meet demands then we miss the purpose of the church.

- Our dreams are important but not when they get in the way of His dream. Our will is important but not when it gets in the way of God's will. Our goal has to be to submit our will and dreams to God's, only then will we succeed.

The Dream, The Domains, The Demands

- The end of my success is that my dreams are fulfilled but the first step to success is this operative word 'demand'.

- The church has become the dreams and destiny capital of the universe when God designed us to be the demand capital of the universe.

- Simply put, we are here to supply what the earth is demanding! So often in our pursuit of wanting to please God, we fall into a trap of religion whereby we become so preoccupied with praying about whether God wants us to do it that we never actually get it done.

- I am not saying that we are here to supply every demand. We fail when we try to succeed at doing everything. Even Jesus knew who He was initially called to supply!

He answered, "I was sent only to the lost sheep of Israel."
Matthew 15:24 (NIV)

- Knowing your field is just as important as the treasure. Dreams help us see a glimpse of the end picture of our lives but to begin the journey of the fulfilment of our dreams we must recognise life's breadcrumbs on the way. These breadcrumbs are called demand

and they will scream to us on the road to success. If we ignore them we are ignoring vital stepping stones that we are going to one day need. So here is the chronology of the treasure in the field principle.

1. What is the Dream- the **final** picture!

_____
_____
_____
_____
_____
_____
_____
_____

2. What is the Domain- the **field** where you have authority and grace.

_____
_____
_____
_____
_____
_____
_____
_____

3. What is the Demand- the **finance** will always be where the need is.

_____
_____
_____
_____
_____
_____
_____
_____

1. Defining The Dream

- The dream is a picture God will give you about the end of your success and what it looks like. Everyone of us will have a dream or a vision that spurns us on. It is a small glimpse at a great future that lives in each one of us and is divinely granted by God.

... And Joseph dreamed a dream, and he told it to his brothers: and they hated him yet the more.
Genesis 37:5

- These divinely granted visions are given without bias. To the saved and the unsaved world. From righteous Joseph all the way to unrighteous Pharaoh.

... And Pharaoh said unto Joseph, I have dreamed a dream, and there is none that can interpret it
Genesis 41:15

- Dreams like parables are God's secrets concealed. They are envisioned glimpses of our future not intended to frustrate us but to give us hope that there is a final outcome.

- When you have a dream or a vision here is what you need to do with it.

Then the LORD replied: "Write down the revelation and make it plain on tablets so that a herald may run with it. For the revelation awaits an appointed time; it speaks of the end and will not prove false. Though it linger, wait for it; it will certainly come and will not delay.
Habakkuk 2:2-3 (NIV)

1. Write it- the bluntest pencil is better than the sharpest mind.
2. Word it- Simplify its meaning to the point that a third party understands what God is asking you to do.
3. Wait for it! The hardest part of any dream or vision is the waiting process. Once you know what you are waiting for then the waiting process isn't all that bad. In fact it actually becomes enjoyable.

- "It speaks of the end!" The reason our dreams and visions frustrate us is because they speak about the future. For some people the glimpse of that future makes the present a prison chamber and the past a cruel prison guard. Understanding that vision speaks of the end should lead us to ask what do we need to do to begin!

- True vision will always have heralds. These are not visionaries but runners. Ambition does it alone, vision from God always requires participation and inclusivity.

- Your vision is your value! It is your greatest piece of real estate. Others will one day pay you for it.

- Spend time waiting on God for his vision for you & write it, word it and learn to prayerfully wait on it.

2. Defining the Domain?

- Blessings are locational! By locational I do not mean purely geographic although that might be the case. Your treasure is in a field and frustration comes when you are trying to find your prosperity when you have not even found your position.

The LORD had said to Abram, "Go from your country, your people and your father's household to the land I will show you."I will make you into a great nation, and I will bless you; I will make your name great, and you will be a blessing.
Genesis 12:1-2

- It is not enough to sacrifice and leave your present domain, you must know the territory within which God will choose to prosper you.

- Your domain may be one or all of three unique values:
  1. Geographic- Location based
  2. Demographic- Statistics based
  3. Psychographic- Behavioural Based

- If the Bible says there is treasure in a field then it is important to know which field holds your treasure.

Joseph had a dream, and when he told it to his brothers, they hated him all the more.
Genesis 37:5

- When Joseph had this dream he was 17 years old. It took 22 years to come to pass and finally manifested at the age of 39. He shared this dream with his brothers in Canaan but what he failed to understand is that the dreams don't happen in our sleep they happen in our domain.

- Dreams don't manifest where you are, they manifest where your domain is. And, the dream or the vision is merely a snapshot of the end picture. It is our duty in the waiting season to spend time prayerfully and strategically mapping out our divine positioning strategy.

- Joseph's brother's hated him because they were not his domain! It is far too easy to assume that where you have the dream is where the dream is supposed to manifest. This is so rarely the truth as so often the old saying rings true that *'a prophet is without honour in his or her own home and among his or her own people'*.

- Joseph's dream would only manifest in the Geography of Egypt, in the demographic of kings and aristocrats and in the psychographic of pagan worshippers.

- Your Geographic begs the question
  "What location has God called me to prosper in?"
- Your Demographic
  " What people group has God called me to prosper in"

- Your Psychographic
  "What are the viable traits of the group God has called me to prosper in."

In the grid below define your Geography, Demography and Psychographic. The more detailed you are in defining them the more likely you are of succeeding. Know them well and live to serve them. For Jesus His Geography was Israel, His Demography was the meek, the poor and the afflicted, His Psychographic was faith!

Vision Brief	1. Geographic	2. Demographic	3. Psychographic
Clothing line	*i.e. Central London*	*i.e. A-B status, senior level management, single, one pet*	*Function over Fashion, trend follower, binge watcher.*

3. Defining the Demand

- Demand is in essence what the treasure is all about!

- Demand is the currency of your dream!

- Never forget this equation it will help you avoid delusions of grandeur

DREAM - DEMAND = DELUSION

- You were put on planet earth to meet a demand!

- Your dreams are demand vacuums in the earth that God has given you the privilege of being His supplier for.

- Unfortunately dreams are like school photos. When you finally line up for those end of year school photos and get the picture the first person and sometimes the only person you are looking out for is yourself.

- Dreams and visions are a snapshot of the end picture. They often depict how God will reward you for supplying the earth with what it needs.

I make known the end from the beginning, from ancient times, what is still to come. I say, 'My purpose will stand, and I will do all that I please.'
Isaiah 46:10 (NIV)

- Demand is the tipping point between my dream and its manifestation and recognising it is why I am in the earth.

"The kingdom of heaven is like treasure hidden in a field. When a man found it, he hid it again, and then in his joy went and sold all he had and bought that field.
Matthew 13:44 (NIV)

- The treasure is the demand, this is why the man hid it again. He knew people wanted it and that he had it in supply.

- Business is the ability to find out what people in my domain want and supply it. Profit is the reward God gives me for serving my domain.

- Demand often reveals itself in the form of commodities. A commodity is a store of value.

- Silver is a commodity because it is a store of value. It does not corrode, it is precious and valuable so people will trade for it.

- Gold likewise is a commodity because it is a store of value.

Other commodities include:

Oil
Coffee
Water
Barley
Digital Information
Houses
Silver
Gold

You: (your voice, your singing, your information, your movies, your songs, your plays, your talks.)

Now we have this treasure in earthen vessels, that the surpassingness of the power may be from God, and not from us,
2 Corinthians 4:7 (BLB)

- These commodities are all storers of wealth over time. In fact the original store of wealth before paper money was silver and gold. Mammon is systemic currency but mammon is not money. We will talk about this in more depth in the chapter (the history and future of money).

- Information is a commodity depending on how you use it to serve or supply your community.

- The only commodity Christ tells us we are not allowed to exploit for gain is salvation and the gifts of the spirit but these too are commodities that are in high demand in our churches today.

- A commodity need not be expensive or rare- just needed. Branding is the ability to make your service known to your domain. In essence your brand communicates to your audience that you have what they need at a price they can afford. You build a brand not based on what you like but what your domain will recognise.

- Many Christians at the stage of demand build a brand that does not communicate to their audience the existence or availability of their ability to supply.

- If you are called to supply something that is already in the earth then find a way to innovate it. Add a value proposition to it- something your domain will get from you that typifies value for money and their time that they can't get from anywhere else.

What is the earth demanding that your dreams are called to supply?

CHAPTER 51 THE TALENTS

Is Kingdom Economy Unfair?

For the kingdom of heaven is as a man travelling into a far country, who called his own servants, and delivered unto them his goods. And unto one he gave five talents, to another two, and to another one; to every man according to his several ability; and straightway took his journey. Then he that had received the five talents went and traded with the same, and made them other five talents. And likewise he that had received two, he also gained other two. But he that had received one went and digged in the earth, and hid his lord's money.

After a long time the lord of those servants cometh, and reckoneth with them. And so he that had received five talents came and brought other five talents, saying, Lord, thou deliveredst unto me five talents: behold, I have gained beside them five talents more. His lord said unto him, Well done, thou good and faithful servant: thou hast been faithful over a few things, I will make thee ruler over many things: enter thou into the joy of thy lord.

He also that had received two talents came and said, Lord, thou deliveredst unto me two talents: behold, I have gained two other talents beside them. His lord said unto him, Well done, good and faithful servant; thou hast been faithful over a few things, I will make thee ruler over many things: enter thou into the joy of thy lord.

Then he which had received the one talent came and said, Lord, I knew thee that thou art an hard man, reaping where thou hast not sown, and gathering where thou hast not strawed: And I was afraid, and went and hid thy talent in the earth: lo, there thou hast that is thine.

His lord answered and said unto him, Thou wicked and slothful servant, thou knewest that I reap where I sowed not, and gather where I have not strawed: Thou oughtest therefore to have put my money to the exchangers, and then at my coming I should have received mine own with usury. Take therefore the talent from him, and give it unto him which hath ten talents. For unto every one that hath shall be given, and he shall have abundance: but from him that hath not shall be taken away even that which he hath.
Matthew 25:14-29 (KJV)

Some authorities say that the **talent** typically weighed about 33 kg (75 lb.) varying from 20 to 40 kg. In February, 2016, the international **price** of gold was about US$1190 per troy ounce. One gram **costs** about $38 (£30.43). At this **price**, a **talent** (33 kg) would be **worth** about $1.25 million (£1,000,925).

- Briefly describe your understanding of this parable?

- It would appear that God has favourites. He gives:

  Person A- £5 Million.
  Person B- £2 Million.
  Person C- £1 Million.

- However the Bible lets us know that he gave to each one "according to his/her ability…"

- The word ability in the New Testament is *dunamis*- it means ability to perform. It is where we get the word dynamic from.

- In the Old Testament the Word for ability to perform is *Koah.*

But remember the LORD your God, for it is he who gives you the ability to produce wealth, and so confirms his covenant, which he swore to your ancestors, as it is today.
Deuteronomy 8:18 (NIV)

- To make wealth takes ability. The word ability means- *competence in doing or skill. A natural aptitude or acquired proficiency.*

- It would appear here that God gave these individuals money according to their level of proficiency and capacity for learning.

In pairs challenge each other and make a list below answering this question based on the one who received from the Lord the least amount of money: Write yourself a cheque for £1,000,000. (or state your own currency). Immerse yourself in the experience of receiving it as you fill in the space.

BANK OF ABUNDANCE

DATE TO CASH MONEY

PAY

TO THE ORDER OF

CURRENCY

DATE SIGNED

⑉000000345⑉ 00300020085⑊ 11000⑉   WWW.FBIMPACT.COM

Now that you have filled in the cheque and received the £1,000,000 making you an unofficial millionaire, fill in the chart below, letting yourself or your partner know how you will invest it.

Item	Cost	Credit Remaining	Return on Investment
i.e. Student Loan	i.e. £10,000	i.e. £990,000	
i.e. house	i.e. £100,000	i.e. £890,000	i.e. £300,000
	Total Cost=	**Total Remaining=**	**Total ROI=**

BANK OF ABUNDANCE

DATE TO CASH MONEY _____

PAY _____

TO THE ORDER OF _____

CURRENCY [ ]

DATE SIGNED _____ _____

⑆000000345⑆ 00300020085⑈ 11000⑆   WWW.FBIMPACT.COM

Write yourself another cheque. This time fill in the blanks and put £100. Immerse yourself again in the experience. Pay attention to how you feel receiving this cheque.

Now in pairs challenge each other and make a list below on your plan of action with this money.

Item	Cost	Credit Remaining	Return on Investment
	Total Cost=	**Total Remaining=**	**Total ROI=**

Learning Outcomes?

1. What did you learn about yourself during this task.

   _____
   _____
   _____
   _____
   _____
   _____
   _____

2. What did you learn about your attitude towards money during this task.

   _____
   _____
   _____
   _____
   _____
   _____
   _____
   _____
   _____
   _____

3. What did you learn about yourself when you had £1,000,000?

   _____
   _____
   _____
   _____
   _____
   _____
   _____

4. What did you learn about yourself when you had £100?

   _____
   _____
   _____
   _____
   _____
   _____
   _____

5. Which of these two tasks was most enjoyable to you? _____

6. Which of these two tasks required more thought from you? _____

Is God a Capitalist?

Capitalism is an economic system based on private ownership of the means of production and their operation for profit. Characteristics central to capitalism include private property, capital accumulation, wage labor, voluntary exchange, a price system, and competitive markets. (Source- Wikipedia)[6]

capitalist
ˈkapɪt(ə)lɪst/
noun
a person who uses their wealth to invest in trade and industry for profit in accordance with the principles of capitalism.

- Capitalism sounds like such a greedy term and rightly so because of what Empires have made of it which is a utilitarian argument that places profit as the ultimate goal and justifying them means of achieving that end.

- However, capitalism in its embryonic form is an economic system that has the service motive and the profit reward!

- When your motive is service (supply) your reward ought to be profit.

For Scripture says, "Do not muzzle an ox while it is treading out the grain," and "The worker deserves his wages."
1 Timothy 5:18 (NIV)

"If you keep your eye on the profit, you're going to skimp on the product. But if you focus on making really great products, then the profits will follow."- Steve Jobs (Co-Founder of Apple)

---

[6] https://en.wikipedia.org/wiki/Capitalism

What We Can glean from this parable

The first law of kingdom economics this parable teaches us is:

> Law 1: The size of your income is the size of your imagination.

- Doing the experiment should have helped you realise that the moment you are presented with even the hypothetical of £1,000,000 that your imagination immediately skyrockets.

- A million pounds makes you think about life through the window of possibilities where as a hundred pound makes you think about life through the window of urgencies. Money doesn't cause the dream but money revives the dream! Or as Solomon put it:

money answereth all things.
Ecclesiastes 10:19 (KJV)

- If Jesus said if we seek the kingdom and his righteousness and we would get all things. Then from what we are learning, the Kingdom gives us access to treasure which we can use as an answer to all things! (what we will eat, what we will wear)

Kingdom= Treasure (open to the righteous and the unrighteous)
Righteousness= Prayer, fasting and giving (in secret)
Things= eat, drink, wear, life's material needs.

- When you receive a Million Pounds you imagine all the things you've always wanted to do. When you receive a hundred Pounds you think of all the things you need to do.

- A million pounds opens the door in the heart to desire but a hundred pounds open the door in the brain to necessity.

> Law 2: The size of your income is the size of your intelligence

- In God's economy you are not given money because you are anointed but because you are able.

- When it comes to the anointing you don't need to be able you need to be available. But when it comes to the kingdom you need to be able and available.

- The anointing only falls on righteous heads, but the kingdom has the righteous and the violent all competing for a share in God's treasure.

From the days of John the Baptist until now, the kingdom of heaven has been subjected to violence, and violent people have been raiding it.
Matthew 11:12 (NIV)

- God apportions wealth based on ability and intelligence regardless of whether you are righteous or wicked. He just commands the church to be righteous about it getting wealth because righteousness safe guards you from the deceitfulness of riches.

But I tell you, love your enemies and pray for those who persecute you, that you may be children of your Father in heaven. He causes his sun to rise on the evil and the good, and sends rain on the righteous and the unrighteous.
Matthew 5:44-45 (NIV)

- The church has been taught a righteousness for rewards message that sadly doesn't fit the bill of grace. Grace is God's unmerited favour! God does not give rewards based on your goodness, He gives rewards based on His Goodness. When it comes to the distribution of wealth, God does not apportion it evenly! He apportions it on the basis of intelligence and ability to steward income.

Of what use is money in the hand of a fool, since he has no intention of acquiring wisdom?
Proverbs 17:16 (NET)

- Did you notice in your a £1000,000 investment how your imagination came alive? Did you notice in your £100 investment how your imagination gave way to your intelligence. In essence you had to think more with £100 investment and less with a £1000,000.

- When it comes to the gospel there are only two types of people: The saved and the unsaved (or as Jesus called them, sheep and goat) when it comes to the kingdom there are only two types of people (the wise and the foolish)

- God sees wealth through the spectacles of wise and foolish not saved and unsaved.

- Anyone can receive this wisdom as God in His grace gives it without condition to anyone who will ask for it.

If any of you lacks wisdom, you should ask God, who gives generously to all without finding fault, and it will be given to you.
James 1:5 (NIV)

- You may begin to ask! "Well, if that's the case, what's the point of being righteous," it would not be a question others in the Bible have not asked when seeing God's economic system.

This is what the wicked are like—
always free of care, they go on amassing wealth. Surely in vain I have kept my heart pure and have washed my hands in innocence. All day long I have been afflicted, and every morning brings new punishments.
Psalm 73:12-14 (NIV)

- Does serving God sometimes make you feel like this scripture? And Why do you think God does this? Before you answer look at the message version of that same verse.

_____
_____

What's going on here? Is God out to lunch? Nobody's tending the store. The wicked get by with everything; they have it made, piling up riches. I've been stupid to play by the rules; what has it gotten me? A long run of bad luck, that's what— a slap in the face every time I walk out the door.
Psalm 73:11-14 (The Message)

> Law 3: God will decrease your income to increase your intelligence!

- You might think in light of what the other two received that the man who only got 1 talent (£1,000,000) was hard done by in comparison.

- However, God is not being cruel to that man, He is merely apportioning wealth to him that he can handle.

- It may not feel like it but the wealth you have is the wealth you can handle!

- Grow your intelligence and you it will automatically grow your income. By intelligence I mean wisdom. Smart people know it all but Intelligent people know one thing or field very well.

- Some of the smartest people in the world are among the poorest people in the world. But a God IQ will always reap financial wealth.

- God was trying to promote the man who received the least by entrusting him with the least. He knew that the only way to increase this mans intelligence was to decrease the mans income.

- Are you in a season right now of seeming financial lack? What if you stopped thinking of it like lack and started thinking of it like divine lack?

- We like to think of God as this wonderful being who only wants to give us good. God wants to do us good but so often His doing us good is based on His allowing us to have bad. James 1:13 clearly states that God does not commit bad but He does permit bad so that there might be good in your end.

"As for you, you meant evil against me, but God meant it for good in order to bring about this present result
Genesis 50:20 (NASB)

- Notice that when Joseph interpreted Pharaoh's dream He showed Him that God was letting him know that there would be seven years of plenty followed by seven years of lack.

> Law 4: Business and Investment is not a calling, We are all called to it. Some are just more lazy than others!

**Seven years of great abundance are coming throughout the land of Egypt, but seven years of famine will follow them. Then all the abundance in Egypt will be forgotten, and the famine will ravage the land. The abundance in the land will not be remembered, because the famine that follows it will be so severe. The reason the dream was given to Pharaoh in two forms is that the matter has been firmly decided by God, and God will do it soon.
Genesis 41:29-32**

- Notice how 7 years of plenty is a season that God will allow Egypt to enjoy plenty and how 7 years of lack is equally a season God will allow Egypt to suffer lack.

- The famine season is an unavoidable part of God's plan and cannot be manipulated.

- Notice again when Joseph was in the prison, no matter what he did, he could not manipulate his prison season to change.

**Within three days Pharaoh will lift up your head and restore you to your position, and you will put Pharaoh's cup in his hand, just as you used to do when you were his cupbearer. I was forcibly carried off from the land of the Hebrews, and even here I have done nothing to deserve being put in a dungeon."But when all goes well with you, remember me and show me kindness; mention me to Pharaoh and get me out of this prison.
Genesis 40:30-15 (NIV)**

- The cup bearer when he was restored forgot all about Joseph and the prophecy he gave in assurance that he would get there.

- Every part of Joseph's life was divinely designed for His good. What if you are in a divinely appointed financial prison?

- What if God has put you here because finally He has got you in a thinking season of your life where now you have to learn economic intelligence?

- God will like Joseph decrease you to increase you!

**"God opposes the proud but shows favour to the humble."
James 4:6 (NIV)**

- Person A invested their money and got a greater level of entrustment.

- Person B the same.

- Person C buried their 1 million and the Lord was so angry He called him "wicked and lazy".

- Wicked means he lacks righteousness. Lazy means he lacks intelligence or the need to go out an get it.

- In the Kingdom God is just as interested in what you do with people as He is with what you do with your money. You cannot be a good steward of people and a bad steward of money because both make a kingdom what a kingdom is.

- The difference Is we love people and use money not the other way around.

- God takes the £1million from Person C and gives it to Person A. This is why the rich get richer!

- God will apportion more to the person who has the most. The most what? Money? No! The most economically intelligent.

- There are three types of income:
  1. Job income- (Time for money economy)
  2. Business Income- (Other Peoples money for time economy)
  3. Opportunity Income- (Risk for reward Economy)

- Lazy People only learn one type of income and therefore they only earn one type of income. Usually this is a job or self employment. Their intelligence teaches them to bury money and not take risks with it because it cost them their time and freedom to get it.

- You cannot serve God and money but you can serve God with money and you need it to truly be of service to God!

- Business and Investments is not a calling! We are all called to it whether we like it or not.

- The moment you step out of your house you are in the world of business. When you go to the grocery shop to buy fruits you are in the calling of business. When you trade your money at the air port you are in the forex market. When you buy a new car you are stepping in to the world of business. When you spend on your credit card or trade in your old phone for cash you are in the world of business. The only difference is which side of the till you choose to position yourself on.

The buyer or the seller
The lender or the borrower
The consumer or the manufacturer
The author or the reader
The inventor or the user
The employer or the employed

- Lazy people are too lazy to want to sit on the other side of the table. It is far too easy to take the rules than to make them. It takes less risk to bury than to believe!

What is your financial goal by the end of:

Year 1?
_____

Year 2?
_____

Year 3?
_____

What are you willing to do to make sure you are sitting on the right side of the table!
_____
_____
_____
_____
_____
_____
_____
_____

CHAPTER 6| FIVE WISE THINGS TO LEARN FROM FIVE FOOLISH VIRGINS

The Parable of the virgins

Then shall the kingdom of heaven be likened unto ten virgins, which took their lamps, and went forth to meet the bridegroom. And five of them were wise, and five *were* **foolish. They that** *were* **foolish took their lamps, and took no oil with them: But the wise took oil in their vessels with their lamps.**

While the bridegroom tarried, they all slumbered and slept. And at midnight there was a cry made, Behold, the bridegroom cometh; go ye out to meet him. Then all those virgins arose, and trimmed their lamps.

And the foolish said unto the wise, Give us of your oil; for our lamps are gone out. But the wise answered, saying, *Not so*; **lest there be not enough for us and you: but go ye rather to them that sell, and buy for yourselves.**

And while they went to buy, the bridegroom came; and they that were ready went in with him to the marriage: and the door was shut. Afterward came also the other virgins, saying, Lord, Lord, open to us. But he answered and said, Verily I say unto you, I know you not. Watch therefore, for ye know neither the day nor the hour wherein the Son of man cometh.
Matthew 25:1-13 (KJV)

Lesson 1| There are only two types of people in the Kingdom: Wise People and Foolish People

- There will always be this strong connection between currency and company!

- If we learn anything from the parable of the virgins it is that bad company corrupts good character but good company corrects bad character.

- In this parable of the Kingdom we see that when it comes to the kingdom, righteousness (virginity) is not the differentiator but wise versus foolish.

- The word foolish here is the Greek word *móros* which is undoubtedly where we derive the term moron from. It means dull, without an edge, mentally inert, nonsensical, acting brainless.

- Its most poignant definition is 'lacking understanding'. This is one of the few parables where the reference is directly to the church. This is indicated to us by use of the word virgin. Virgin here is a symbol for righteousness or holiness of some sort. However, when it comes to the kingdom purity alone is not the qualifying mark.

- The word *móros* comes from the base word *musterion*. This is where we get the word mystery from. It literally means a mystery or secret doctrine of which initiation is necessary.

- So when it says 5 were foolish, it simply means 5 christians lacked an ability to understand the mysteries or secret doctrines of the Kingdom hidden in the parables.

- The Kingdom reveals the secret will of God based not on righteousness but on wisdom! You're ability to unlock this doctrine will reveal to you treasures of the Kingdom that others (sadly within the church) may not understand.

Lesson 2| You are only as wise as the five wisest people you choose to put in your life!

- Five wise people were labeled wise because they chose to associate with four people wiser than them.

- Five foolish people were known by the four other foolish people they chose to associate with.

- Friendship is a choice. You don't make friends you choose them. Successful people associate with successful people.

- There is no such thing as success by mistake, there is only success by association!

Blessed is the one who does not walk in step with the wicked or stand in the way that sinners take or sit in the company of mockers
Psalm 1:1 (NIV)

- Is it possible to be guilty by association? If so then it is equally possible to be successful by association.

- In the Bible we see a woman called Ruth go from uneducated, poor and bereaved to one of the most successful female entrepreneurs of scripture simply by association.

But Ruth replied, "Don't urge me to leave you or to turn back from you. Where you go I will go, and where you stay I will stay. Your people will be my people and your God my God.
Ruth 1:16 (NIV)

- This powerful statement came at a cost. She would have to let go of her best friend Orpah to follow her God friend Naomi.

- Many fail the journey of success simply upon choosing the right passengers alone.

- RUTH in Hebrew means:

A female associate
Friend
Mate
Neighbour

It comes from the root word ra'ah

It means:

To break
Keep company with

- Ruth's name alone is the most important part of the text because it literally means to break up to make up. What if what's stopping you from moving into new company is old company? The daunting fact that some of your best company is family but there can be no breakthrough without a break up and divine set up without an upset.

- Orpah in Hebrew means stubborn or stiff-necked. It occurs 33 times in the Old Testament. In Exodus 33 God says to Israel that He won't go with them because they are Orpah (stiff necked)

- What if Orpah's are good people that just don't want the kind of success that you want? What if they are just not expecting the same thing from life that you are?

- What if God can't bless you because of who you're trying to take with you? Here's an experiment to help you find out. The purpose of this experiment is to help you prioritise your friends.

- Find on the next page a table. On it write your top 30 friends from your mobile phone book. In the right box put a tick next to the ones you consider wiser than you and that you can look up to. These ticks must represent people in your life who you learn from, directional influencers in your life that drive you towards your ultimate goal in life. If you find this activation difficult perhaps it is time to make wiser choices and rewrite your list based on where you are going and who you want to be.

FRIENDS (Name)	WISE FRIENDS (Tick)

FRIENDS (Name)	WISE FRIENDS (Tick)

Lesson 3| Your friend Will determine your end.

- The last three letters of friend should serve as an indication of their purpose in your life.

- See where they are and ask yourself if you want to be there! You're true friends are either where you want to be or facing that direction.

- Five wise people all ended up in the same place. Five foolish people equally ended up in the same place.

- When it comes to the kingdom, you do not make friends you choose them.

- In the grid below choose five people (possibly not on your phone book) who their end reminds you of where you wan to end. They could be a boss at work, a successful author, a brilliant business man you know. Decide for yourself when you are going to call them to let them know that you want to glean from them. Meet with them, get to know them, ask them for mentoring and guidance. (Not for money! Their time is way more valuable!)

FRIENDS (Name)	WHEN WILL YOU CALL THEM?

**Without counsel plans fail, but with many advisers they succeed.
Proverbs 15:22 (ESV)**

Lesson 4| It is foolish to go through Life with a Lamp and nothing to Light it.

- The great thing about foolish people is they always give themselves away from the beginning.

- We call these give aways red flags!

- The red flag that the wise virgins were quick to recognise was that the foolish ones wanted to borrow oil they've never had to pay the price for like the wise did.

- Foolish people live their lives through yours!

- They don't ever feel responsibility to buy fuel when they can simply borrow yours.

- Here are some red flags to watch out for!

RED FLAG 1
Do you find it difficult to say no even to people closest to you?

RED FLAG 2
Is pleasing people more important to you than taking care of yourself?

RED FLAG 3
Do others navigate towards you for how you can help them or for what you can do for them?

RED FLAG 4
Does your friend rejoice in your accomplishments or are they quick to dismiss it?

RED FLAG 5
Do you have someone in your life who says words like: "Without me you're nothing", "Don't forget all the things I have done for you!" "If you do that I'm out!"

RED FLAG 6
Does you telling them you can't result in some form of control i.e. silent treatment, anger, avoidance etc.

- Remember not all these red flags are intended to make you fire people from your life but wisely adjust your boundaries to allow them to know where you begin and they end. Don't let others abuse you by spending you're oil to keep their lights on.

Lesson 5| Wise and Foolish People sleep two different types of sleep

A wise youth harvests in the summer, but one who sleeps during harvest is a disgrace.
Proverbs 10:5 (NLT)

- Know what season you are in by being ready at all seasons.

be prepared in season and out of season
2 Timothy 4:2 (NIV)

- Wise people and foolish people sleep two different types of sleep. Wise people sleep blissfully whilst fools sleep wishfully.

- Wise people have prepared well to perform well whereas fools live with an entitled expectation that someone else is going to help them get through the next season of their life and this is just not the case.

CHAPTER 71 THE PRODIGAL SON

And he said, "There was a man who had two sons. And the younger of them said to his father, 'Father, give me the share of property that is coming to me.' And he divided his property between them. Not many days later, the younger son gathered all he had and took a journey into a far country, and there he squandered his property in reckless living. And when he had spent everything, a severe famine arose in that country, and he began to be in need. So he went and hired himself out to one of the citizens of that country, who sent him into his fields to feed pigs. And he was longing to be fed with the pods that the pigs ate, and no one gave him anything.

"But when he came to himself, he said, 'How many of my father's hired servants have more than enough bread, but I perish here with hunger! I will arise and go to my father, and I will say to him, "Father, I have sinned against heaven and before you. I am no longer worthy to be called your son. Treat me as one of your hired servants."' And he arose and came to his father. But while he was still a long way off, his father saw him and felt compassion, and ran and embraced him and kissed him. And the son said to him, 'Father, I have sinned against heaven and before you. I am no longer worthy to be called your son.' But the father said to his servants, 'Bring quickly the best robe, and put it on him, and put a ring on his hand, and shoes on his feet. And bring the fattened calf and kill it, and let us eat and celebrate. For this my son was dead, and is alive again; he was lost, and is found.' And they began to celebrate.

"Now his older son was in the field, and as he came and drew near to the house, he heard music and dancing. And he called one of the servants and asked what these things meant. And he said to him, 'Your brother has come, and your father has killed the fattened calf, because he has received him back safe and sound.' But he was angry and refused to go in. His father came out and entreated him, but he answered his father, 'Look, these many years I have served you, and I never disobeyed your command, yet you never gave me a young goat, that I might celebrate with my friends. But when this son of yours came, who has devoured your property with prostitutes, you killed the fattened calf for him!' And he said to him, 'Son, you are always with me, and all that is mine is yours. It was fitting to celebrate and be glad, for this your brother was dead, and is alive; he was lost, and is found.'"
Matthew 15:11-32 (ESV)

Why God isn't giving you the amount of money you asked Him for!

- Have you ever asked God to:
  a. Make you rich?
  b. Make you a millionaire?
  c. Give you a specific amount of money?

- This particular parable is proof of another hidden kingdom truth: "Money has a twin sister called motive!"

When you ask, you do not receive, because you ask with wrong motives, that you may spend what you get on your pleasures.
James 4:2-3 (NIV)

- God will always give you and I the money He knows we are able to handle! (Or as in the previous chapter- the size of your income is the size of your intelligence.)

- Some people do not know how sinful they are until they get money. The connection between the heart (seat of passions) and money is so strong that they Bible says a man or woman's heart resides where their treasure is.

For where your treasure is, there your heart will be also.
Luke 12:34 (NIV)

* Treasure and heart, like money and motive are strongly connected. Money doesn't change people, it amplifies parts of people that were always there.

* Was the prodigal son addicted to sexual immorality- no! Because an addiction cannot be kicked, as soon as this man's money ran out so did his immorality!

* Addictions are those things that we would rob our grand mother to get a hold of! What the prodigal son likely suffered with (even though the text does not tell us so) was loneliness and a void he thought money could pay for and fill. Money possibly amplified his preexistent need for companionship.

* The Bible says of what use is money in the hands of a fool because he has no desire to get wisdom- (Proverbs 17:16)

* God will not give you wealth you are not wise enough for, that's satan's job.

* Wealth without wisdom is not a blessing it is a miserable curse.

* When satan makes men rich, he fills their houses with the deceitfulness of riches. This is why you can have a lot of money and be in rehab for depression, anxiety, alcohol and substance abuse. The devil offers currency at great cost!

For what is a man profited, if he shall gain the whole world, and lose his own soul? or what shall a man give in exchange for his soul?
Matthew 16:26 KJV)

- This is what the Bible means by not being able to serve both God and mammon. It is not trying to deny the church the ability to have both God and money but mammon is a spirit that causes money to be ill gotten and not blessed at the end.

Dishonest money dwindles away, but whoever gathers money little by little makes it grow.
Proverbs 13:11 (NIV)

- Repeat this prayer:

Father,

I repent of asking you for more wealth instead of more wisdom. Thank you for giving me the amount of money you can trust me with. Lord I don't intend to stay on this level of finances. Increase my economic intelligence that my economy might be expanded. Father in the Name of your Son Jesus Christ grant me a wise and understanding heart so that I will know that it is you who gives the ability to get wealth.

In Jesus Name,

Amen.

The winning lotto ticket ruined my life!

Kenneth and Connie Parker, who won $25 million, divorced just months after "striking it rich."

After William Post won $16.2 million in a Pennsylvania lottery in 1988 his brother tried to hire a contract killer to hit him and his wife. When he declared bankruptcy in 1993 he said, "Everybody dreams of winning money, but nobody realises the nightmares that come out of the woodwork, or the problems." When he died in 2006 he was living on his meagre monthly Social Security check and The Washington Post headlined his obituary "The Unhappy Lottery Winner."

Ken Proxmire, who won $1 million in a Michigan lottery, was bankrupt within five years.

Charles Riddle, who won $1 million in Michigan in 1975, got divorced, faced several lawsuits, and was indicted for selling cocaine.

After Juan Rodriguez won $149 million in a New York lottery, his wife of 17 years filed for divorce and took half of his winnings.

After Lewis Snipes' wife won $31.5 million in 1988, her husband disagreed with her and her sisters over whether to accept the lump sum payout. The matter was litigated for four years and split the family apart.

Thomas Strong, who won $3 million in a Texas lottery in 1993, died in a shoot-out with police in 2006.

Shefik Tallmadge, who won $6.7 million in the Arizona lottery in 1988, declared bankruptcy in 2005.

Rhoda Toth, who, together with her husband Alex, won $13 million in 1990, is in prison for income tax fraud. Within two years after hitting the lottery jackpot, the Toths were borrowing money to pay bills and were living in a trailer without electricity. In 2008, Alex died "hating life" and Rhoda pled guilty to filing false tax returns and was sentenced to two years in prison. She says, "The winning ticket ruined my life."

Jack Whittaker, who won $314 million in a lottery in December 2002, has been sued for bouncing checks at a casino, was divorced by his wife, was ordered to undergo rehab because of drunken driving, was sued by the father of a teenager who was found dead in one of Whittaker's houses, and took to drink. And he had pampered his teenage granddaughter, Brandi Bragg, with four new cars and a $2000 a week allowance, she died of a drug overdose. Whittaker's ex-wife, Jewell, said, "If I knew what was going to transpire, honestly, I would have torn the ticket up." In July 2009 Brandi's mother, Ginger, was found dead at age 42.

Victoria Zell, who shared an $11 million Powerball jackpot with her husband in 2001, was penniless by 2006 and serving seven years in a Minnesota prison, having been convicted in a drug- and alcohol-induced collision that killed someone.

Abraham Shakespeare, who received $13 million from the Florida state lottery in 2006, spent the money in a little over two years and was murdered by someone who was probably one of his newfound "friends." His relatives said that he was "miserable early on from his newfound fortune" ("Trust was costly for Shakespeare," The Tampa Tribune, Feb. 4, 2010). In January 2007 he purchased a million-dollar home and then sold it for a loss of $350,000 two years later to a woman who said that she wanted to write the story of his life. In January 2010 Shakespeare's body was found buried under a slab of concrete on the property.

- There is no fast food restaurant to financial well being and if you rush your way to it you will fall into temptation.

People who want to get rich fall into temptation and a trap and into many foolish and harmful desires that plunge men into ruin and destruction
1Timothy 6:9 (NIV)

- Without the law you do not know wisdom and without wisdom money will be a burden to you and no longer a blessing.

Do not trust in extortion or take pride in stolen goods; though your riches increase, do not set your heart on them.
Psalm 62:10 (NIV)

- Remember, if money is too big to walk away from you will inevitably end up being a in compromise and service to mammon.

- It is far too easy to submit your life to a self justifying spirit of mammon which is based in fraud, employment fraud, false identification, laundering, embezzling, tax fraud or avoidance, bribery, insurance scams, gambling, bribery, credit card fraud and the such.

**A greedy man brings trouble to his family, but he who hates bribes will live
Proverbs 15:27(NIV)**

- The law of God is the wisdom of God. Once you have it you won't need to seek riches, riches will seek you!

**Do not wear yourself out to get rich; have wisdom and show restraint
Proverbs 23:4 (NIV)**

Is your desire to get rich as strong as your desire to get blessed?

In groups or on you own discuss and evaluate this question.

_____
_____
_____
_____
_____
_____
_____

The blessing of the LORD, it maketh rich, and he addeth no sorrow with it.
Proverbs 10:22 (KJV)

- The Word blessing finds it roots in the Hebrew culture. It is more than just a benediction but an action.

- The Hebrew word for bless is the word *'Barak'*.

- God confers His *Barak* upon Adam and Eve in Genesis 1:26 where He says:

God blessed them and said to them, "Be fruitful and increase in number; fill the earth and subdue it. Rule over the fish in the sea and the birds in the sky and over every living creature that moves on the ground."
Genesis 1:28 (NIV)

- It is important at this point to mention that the blessing is not what was said, the blessing empowered and enforced what was said. Which is why God blessed them and said!

- The word Barak means to kneel as though in worship.

- When God was performing a Barak to Adam, He was conferring authority to Adam in the sight of all creation. He was not saying He was equal with Adam but Rather that He was equivalent to Adam. Since Adam was God's image, God was demonstrating to creation to respect Adam as creation respects God. When Adam fell from that glory (image) creation no longer needed to.

- In Christ however the church is in a new barak season where that blessing once again makes rich and adds no sorrow.

Praise be to the God and Father of our Lord Jesus Christ, who has blessed us in the heavenly realms with every spiritual blessing in Christ.
Ephesians 1:3 (NIV)

- So powerful is the blessing, that we see in the Old Testament two brothers fighting not over money but who was going to get words!

Esau said, "Isn't he rightly named Jacob? This is the second time he has taken advantage of me: He took my birthright, and now he's taken my blessing!" Then he asked, "Haven't you reserved any blessing for me?"
Genesis 27:36 (NIV)

- Jacob so understood the legal power of the blessing that he stole it from his older brother and lived a fully blessed life wherever he went.

- When you understand that you are blessed you will prosper in any environment God takes you through. That Jesus on the cross died to *Barak* you and confer honour that you had lost back to you, you will not settle for less.

- What many fail to realise about Genesis 1:26 is that God blessed the man of the spirit. I call this the fourth dimensional man! Christians are so much more dynamic than we could ever possibly imagine. We are no longer mere humans the day we give our lives to Christ- The Bible calls us New Creatures. It is from this new creation that we can literally create wealth. We will talk about this in the next Chapter.

Therefore, if anyone is in Christ, the new creation has come: The old has gone, the new is here!
2 Corinthians 5:17 (NIV)

CHAPTER 8| KOSMOS VERSUS KINGDOM

- You have undoubtedly heard the term, living within your means. In this teaching you will learn how to live and operate within your dimension. As a Christian believer, you are more dynamic than you can ever possibly imagine. You are so much more than a three dimensional being- God has added a fourth dimension to you and it is from this dimension that you experience God's divine authority.

Why satan tried to kill Jesus, Judas and Job

- It would seem that satan has a kill list for anyone who had the letter J in their name. These three characters in the Bible had personal encounters with satan himself. Besides the common denominator in their name, what made these three characters so enticing to satan that he couldn't simply send one of his demonic spirits or ignore them?

- These three characters all had two things that made them a threat
  1. Righteousness
  2. Money

- This lethal combination of purity and prosperity made them too threatening to the enemy to be ignored.

- The devil does not mind anyone having a lot of money as long as they have a bankrupt soul.

- The world is yet to see the power of a Christian believer totally prosperous and totally surrendered to the Holy Spirit. The day that happens, the devil himself will stand as an opponent against such a unique tribe. A truly Melchizedek tribe!

- Job was righteous and rich:

There was a man in the country of Uz named Job. He was a man of perfect integrity, who feared God and turned away from evil. He had seven sons and three daughters. His estate included 7,000 sheep, 3,000 camels, 500 yoke of oxen, 500 female donkeys, and a very large number of servants. Job was the greatest man among all the people of the east.
Job 1:1 (HCSB)

- The devil was enticed by his perfect integrity. He simply could not be bought!

One day the angels came to present themselves before the LORD, and Satan also came with them. The LORD said to Satan, "Where have you come from?" Satan answered the LORD, "From roaming throughout the earth, going back and forth on it." Then the LORD said to Satan, "Have you considered my servant Job? There is no one on earth like him; he is blameless and upright, a man who fears God and shuns evil." "Does Job fear God for nothing?" Satan replied. "Have you not put a hedge around him and his household and everything he has? You have blessed the work of his hands, so that his flocks and herds are spread throughout the land. But now stretch out your hand and strike everything he has, and he will surely curse you to your face."
Job 1:6-11 (NIV)

- The Lord was not just protecting Job but also protecting Job's possessions. Satan recognises God's provision over Job's life and Job's possessions. That means the Lord is protecting not just you but your car, your house, your television, your computer. God has an insurance policy from infringement over you and your stuff.

- The devil made a wager with God that if God would touch Job's possessions then Job would lose his righteousness.

- Jesus was so full of wealth that He did not just own it, the Bible says He commanded it! He never even paid taxes from within His own ministry, he paid taxes through decreeing the money to just show up!

go to the lake and throw out your line. Take the first fish you catch; open its mouth and you will find a four-drachma coin. Take it and give it to them for my tax and yours."
Matthew 17:27 (NIV)

- Again, the devil himself shows up to Jesus on top of a mountain and even tries to barter with him. He shows Jesus the glory of the earth realm that he owns in the twinkling of an eye. Jesus sees all of Satan's wealth, resources, earthly kings (not righteous), ungodly multitude. Satan then offers Jesus all of the earthly kingdoms and the riches (glory) they have if only Jesus would bow down to Him and submit over His Heavenly Kingdom for all the earthly kingdoms. Jesus is tempted but refuses the offer recognising all earthly kingdoms as pale in comparison to the riches of His Father's glory that adds no sorrow!

Again, the devil took him to a very high mountain and showed him all the kingdoms of the world and their splendour. "All this I will give you," he said, "if you will bow down and worship me."
Matthew 4:8-9 (NIV)

- The devil opposed and tried to contaminate the integrity of these three characters but only succeeded with one. Judas! For whom the love of money and the deceitfulness of riches was too overwhelming and caused Him to sell our Messiah for the price of a slave.

When Judas, who had betrayed him, saw that Jesus was condemned, he was seized with remorse and returned the thirty pieces of silver to the chief priests and the elders."I have sinned," he said, "for I have betrayed innocent blood." "What is that

to us?" they replied. "That's your responsibility." So Judas threw the money into the temple and left. Then he went away and hanged himself.
Matthew 27:3-5

- What bewitched Judas to do such an act and then immediately regret his decision?

Then Satan entered Judas, called Iscariot, one of the Twelve. And Judas went to the chief priests and the officers of the temple guard and discussed with them how he might betray Jesus.
Luke 22:3-4 (NIV)

- What if this entire cosmic battle is one not just for souls but for source? What if money and souls are the make up of a divine kingdom and satan wants you to use souls and love money instead of loving souls and using money?

- What if the blinders are on the eyes of the church that we can't see the connect between hearts and money? The reason satan's ministry is succeeding is because he has the money to buy back what Jesus purchased by His blood! People every day are selling their souls to reach their purpose, all under the illusion that they will be happy on the other side failing to realise that the grass may be greener on the other side but so is the water bill!

- What if the greatest end time harvest of souls will begin when a wealth transfer revival finally hits the church and we start reaping the riches that were always ours? The end result of this wealth transfer will automatically be souls because hearts always follow treasure.

For where your treasure is, there your heart will be also.
Luke 12:34 (NIV)

- Satan is afraid of the day righteous people get rich because they will lead government without compromise and lies, they will run businesses with integrity, they will make movies that tell righteous stories, they will sing songs that glorify God and not sex, drugs or money, they will lead their families because their parents will be home and not having to work two jobs- leaving parenting to the television screen, they will teach their children the ways of the Lord because they are too righteous to compromise and too rich to be bought!

Who is Satan?

- Satan has many definitions in the Bible. Each title reveals a little bit about his strategy in the earth. Can you write down below what his potential strategy might be for the following titles. He is called:

1. The prince of the power of the air

_____
_____
_____
_____
_____
_____

2. He is called Lucifer (meaning star)

_____
_____
_____
_____
_____
_____

3. He is called satan (accuser) Job 2:2, Revelation 12:10

_____
_____
_____
_____
_____
_____

Prince of the power of the air- symbolises to us his desire to control the airways. He wants complete air control. His fight for this is demonstrated in media and entertainment. His strategy to rule the air is propagated mostly from this arena. His rule over the atmosphere is anything anti Christ. He hates worship, praise or any other godly sound because they break his strong hold.

Lucifer- Any marketer knows that if you want to be successful you need brand ambassadors. In the marketing world these are called 'influencers'. Satan works with people to give them fame at the cost of their soul. Very few people start out in the music industry wanting to do drugs, or sing about their sexual escapades. Most start out wanting to express their God given creativity only to realise that the air is so controlled in Hollywood that the only way in is to follow the pattern of the air. Some naive believe they can compromise and change the air once they are inside only to realise that compromise only leads to more compromise and that once you sell your soul for fame it is very difficult to get it back. God has stars and God makes famous but Satan's stars pay a deer price. Shiny as stars they may appear, without the media these stars are only presenting a false sense of light!

**AND NO WONDER, FOR SATAN HIMSELF MASQUERADES AS AN ANGEL OF LIGHT.
IT IS NOT SURPRISING, THEN, IF HIS SERVANTS ALSO MASQUERADE AS SERVANTS OF RIGHTEOUSNESS. THEIR END WILL BE WHAT THEIR ACTIONS DESERVE.
2 CORINTHIANS 11:14-15 (NIV)**

The Accuser- The devil is a legalist. He Himself is under the law and not under grace. He uses God's word to accuse people and bring them into guilt, shame and fear. We defeat the enemy not by law but by grace (an understanding of where we stand in God and His total love for us equips us to fight the enemy and win because we are fighting from a completely different arena of strength). Satan's fight is from a place without redemption, our fight is from a place with redemption by His blood.

**THEY TRIUMPHED OVER HIM BY THE BLOOD OF THE LAMB AND BY THE WORD OF THEIR TESTIMONY; THEY DID NOT LOVE THEIR LIVES SO MUCH AS TO SHRINK FROM DEATH.
REVELATION 12:11 (NIV)**

- The definition I will be focusing on for the devil is **god of this world.**

**IN THEIR CASE THE GOD OF THIS WORLD HAS BLINDED THE MINDS OF THE UNBELIEVERS, TO KEEP THEM FROM SEEING THE LIGHT OF THE GOSPEL OF THE GLORY OF CHRIST, WHO IS THE IMAGE OF GOD.
2 CORINTHIANS 4:4 (ESV)**

- The devil is known as the god of this world whose function is to blind eyes so that no one will believe the gospel of the glory of Christ.

- Know that here his job is two fold:
1. That unbelievers stay in unbelief and carry on in their intellectual, agnostic or atheist ways.
2. That no one will believe the gospel of the "GLORY" of Christ

- Our Messiah is not just anointed, He is glorious! The word glory means 'full of wealth and splendour'. In essence He is the epitome of wealth of righteousness and riches combined.

The anointing Versus the glory

- So often we hear the word anointing and glory being used interchangeably to describe the supernatural power of God. Whilst we are right that the anointing is the power of God, the glory is not the power of God!

- The anointing is the power of God, the glory is the splendour of God!

- The power brings action the glory brings adoration!

- The power is received the glory is beheld!

- God's power is an act of His kindness but God's glory is the act of His goodness!

- God's power works through you to demonstrate God's love to others. God's Glory works in you to demonstrate God's goodness to you!

Then Moses said, "Now show me your glory." And the LORD said, "I will cause all my goodness to pass in front of you, and I will proclaim my name, the LORD, in your presence.
Exodus 33:18-19 (NIV)

- God's power is invisible with manifest tangible results, God's glory is visible manifestation of His goodness.

- A more succinct definition of the difference between the anointing on your life and the glory on your life can be found in the book of Isaiah 60 and Isaiah 61 where the difference is clear to see.

The Spirit of the Sovereign Lord is on me, because the Lord has anointed me to proclaim good news to the poor. He has sent me to bind up the brokenhearted, to proclaim freedom for the captives and release from darkness for the prisoners, To proclaim the year of the Lord's favour and the day of vengeance of our God, to comfort all who mourn, and provide for those who grieve in Zion— to bestow on them a crown of beauty instead of ashes, the oil of joy instead of mourning, and a garment of praise instead of a spirit of despair. They will be called oaks of righteousness, a planting of the Lord for the display of his splendour. They will rebuild the ancient ruins and restore the places long devastated; they will renew the ruined cities that have been devastated for generations. Strangers will shepherd your flocks; foreigners will work your fields and vineyards. And you will be called priests of the Lord, you will be named ministers of our God. You will feed on the wealth of nations, and in their riches you will boast. Instead of your shame you will receive a double portion, and instead of disgrace you will rejoice in your inheritance. And so you will inherit a double portion in your land, and everlasting joy will be yours. "For I, the Lord, love justice; I hate robbery and wrongdoing. In my faithfulness I will reward my people and make an everlasting covenant with them. Their descendants will be known among the nations and their offspring among the peoples. All who see them will acknowledge that they are a people the Lord has blessed." I delight greatly in the Lord; my soul rejoices in my God. For he has clothed me with garments of salvation and arrayed me in a robe of his righteousness, as a bridegroom adorns his head like a priest, and as a bride adorns

herself with her jewels. For as the soil makes the sprout come up and a garden causes seeds to grow, so the Sovereign Lord will make righteousness and praise spring up before all nations.
Isaiah 61:1-11 (NIV)

"Arise, shine, for your light has come, and the glory of the Lord rises upon you. See, darkness covers the earth and thick darkness is over the peoples, but the Lord rises upon you and his glory appears over you. Nations will come to your light, and kings to the brightness of your dawn. "Lift up your eyes and look about you: All assemble and come to you; your sons come from afar, and your daughters are carried on the hip. Then you will look and be radiant, your heart will throb and swell with joy; the wealth on the seas will be brought to you, to you the riches of the nations will come. Herds of camels will cover your land, young camels of Midian and Ephah. And all from Sheba will come, bearing gold and incense and proclaiming the praise of the Lord. All Kedar's flocks will be gathered to you, the rams of Nebaioth will serve you; they will be accepted as offerings on my altar, and I will adorn my glorious temple. "Who are these that fly along like clouds, like doves to their nests? Surely the islands look to me; in the lead are the ships of Tarshish, bringing your children from afar, with their silver and gold, to the honour of the Lord your God, the Holy One of Israel, for he has endowed you with splendour. "Foreigners will rebuild your walls, and their kings will serve you. Though in anger I struck you, in favour I will show you compassion. Your gates will always stand open, they will never be shut, day or night, so that people may bring you the wealth of the nations— their kings led in triumphal procession. For the nation or kingdom that will not serve you will perish; it will be utterly ruined. "The glory of Lebanon will come to you, the juniper, the fir and the cypress together, to adorn my sanctuary; and I will glorify the place for my feet. The children of your oppressors will come bowing before you; all who despise you will bow down at your feet and will call you the City of the Lord, Zion of the Holy One of Israel. "Although you have been forsaken and hated, with no one traveling through, I will make you the everlasting pride and the joy of all generations. You will drink the milk of nations and be nursed at royal breasts. Then you will know that I, the Lord, am your Saviour, your Redeemer, the Mighty One of Jacob. Instead of bronze I will bring you gold, and silver in place of iron. Instead of wood I will bring you bronze, and iron in place of stones. I will make peace your governor and well-being your ruler. No longer will violence be heard in your land, nor ruin or destruction within your borders, but you will call your walls Salvation and your gates Praise. The sun will no more be your light by day, nor will the brightness of the moon shine on you, for the Lord will be your everlasting light, and your God will be your glory. Your sun will never set again, and your moon will wane no more; the Lord will be your everlasting light, and your days of sorrow will end. Then all your people will be righteous and they will possess the land forever. They are the shoot I have planted, the work of my hands, for the display of my splendour. The least of you will become a thousand, the smallest a mighty nation. I am the Lord; in its time I will do this swiftly."
Isaiah 60:1-22 (NIV)

ANOINTING	GLORY
Gospel Message	Kingdom Message
Poor is the audience (those in need)	Nations come to you
Liberty to captives	Kings come to you
Prisoners	You will be radiant and full of light
Mourners	Wealth will come to you
Grievers	Riches of Nations will come to you
Beauty for Ashes	Herds and camels cover your land
the Spirit of despair	Gold will come to you
Rebuilding ruins	They will bring silver and gold to honour the Lord
Renew ruined Cities	Kings will serve you
Priests of the Lord	Gates will never shut so people can bring their wealth
Ministers of God	God will make you an everlasting pride

- The anointing brings around you those that have needs and the glory brings around you those that have resources.

- The anointing equips you to preach the gospel with power. The glory equips you to be the gospel as a testament of His divine goodness!

- The anointing allows you to demonstrate an invisible kingdom to convince others to believe. The glory allows you to be a living demonstration and to be His visible kingdom that cannot be hidden.

- Anointing is for work, glory is for rest!

Therefore my heart is glad, and my glory rejoiceth: my flesh also shall rest in hope. Psalm 16:9 (KJV)

- God's glory is light! (arise, shine for your light has come). The ultimate assignment of the enemy is to stop people from seeing the light of the glory of the gospel. The gospel is good news not just of healing but of splendour, wealth and resources that the devil does not want you to see.

**In their case the god of this world has blinded the minds of the unbelievers, to keep them from seeing the light of the gospel of the glory of Christ, who is the image of God.
2 Corinthians 4:4 (ESV)**

What is the job of the god of this world?

- The job of the devil is to keep us in darkness concerning the gospel and the glory of the gospel.

- His ultimate goal is ignorance. That unbelievers don't believe in Jesus and believers don't believe that Jesus wants to be good now.

Beloved, I wish above all things that thou mayest prosper and be in health, even as thy soul prospereth.
3 John 1:2 (KJV)

- God wants us to prosper, be healthy and spiritually sound. The enemy wants the unsaved to be ungodly and the godly to be be poor. Christ doesn't give us life or godliness He gives us the promise of life and godliness.

According as his divine power hath given unto us all things that pertain unto life and godliness, through the knowledge of him that hath called us to glory and virtue:
2 Peter 1:3 (KJV)

- God has given the church more than just a duty to be virtuous and righteous, He has also called us to glory (splendour, wealth, majesty). He has not just called us to godliness but to He has also called us to life.

- The word for world is the Greek word *kosmos* it is where we get the word cosmology (study of the universe or things that appear) or the word cosmetics (make up, fashion) from.

- Other definitions include

1. Worldly affairs
2. Inhabitants of the world
3. adornment
4. constitution
5. ungodly people
6. World systems

- In essence satan is the god of cosmetic holiness, cosmetic christianity, cosmetic religion, cosmetic money, etc. He is the god of worldly arrangements- written and unwritten laws.

- He keeps the world ticking through a system of currency Biblically known as mammon.

- Mammon is not money it is currency! Mammon is cosmetic money!

- Mammon is not the flesh, the eyes or life, mammon is the lust of the flesh, the lust of the eyes and the pride of life.

For everything in the world--the lust of the flesh, the lust of the eyes, and the pride of life--comes not from the Father but from the world.
1 John 1:26 (NIV)

- True money belongs to the Lord! Fake money (or currency) belongs to the systems of the world that it is the devils job to operate. We call this currency fiat money, the Bible refers to it as mammon. We will talk about this in greater detail in the next chapter (the difference between money and currency)

- Satan's job is not chaos but order but if chaos brings order he is willing to do whatever it takes to shift things in his favour. For the devil it is all about money! He knows that the each coin he gathers is attached to a soul he can force and bend to his will. Every evil thing imaginable is rooted in the love of money- from every government scandal to every marital divorce, you can guarantee the lack or the abundance of money had something to do with it.

For the love of money is the root of all evil: which while some coveted after, they have erred from the faith, and pierced themselves through with many sorrows.
1 Timothy 6:10 (KJV)

- The spirit of religion comes in at this point and convinces many Christians that money is evil. You must be careful to thoroughly understand that this is an intended plan to keep the church in a 'vision with no provision' place. The lack of money is just as dangerous and evil as the love of money!

- Satan's economy is not an employment based system but an enslavement based system. God is an employer, satan is an enslaver! The difference is satan gives you a job but God gives you a work! This is why Jesus said:

I must work the works of him that sent me, while it is day: the night cometh, when no man can work.
John 9:4 (KJV

- A job is not work! Work is what God gave Adam in the garden. God made birds to fly! This means when a bird flies it is working. God made fish to swim, when a fish swims it is working. God made Michael Jordan to play basketball; when Michael Jordan plays basketball he is working!

- The difference between your work and you job can be found in the grid on the next page. You might want to help yourself in teams by inserting some of your own differences.

JOB	WORK
What I am paid for	What I am made for
What I do	Who I am
Makes me tired	Gives me strength
Income Source	Identity Source
What Pays me	What Pains me
I can be fired	I can't be fired
My Wage	My Worth
Feeds your mouth	Feeds your soul

- Your worth is your work! When you find it, you find your greatest value and no one can rob you of it. Satan will rob you of your work by giving you a job. Don't let your job suffocate your work!

"Do not work for the food which perishes, but for the food which endures to eternal life, which the Son of Man will give to you, for on Him the Father, God, has set His seal."
John 6:27 (NASB)

- In Satan's order you are enslaved by a system that robs you of your greatest commodity- time! Time is your greatest currency simply because it is irreplaceable. There are only two things you can do with time
  1. Spend it!
  2. Waste it!

- Satan wants you to waste your time away because he knows he is running out of it. Like a parasite he wants to live as long as he can, even if he knows that living is through you!

Therefore, rejoice, O heavens and you who dwell in them! But woe to you, O earth and sea, for the devil has come down to you in great wrath, because he knows that his time is short!"
Revelation 12:2 (ESV)

- This time for money scheme has been satan's economic structure since the book of Exodus. Under this scheme, humanity is reduced to slave horses with carrots dangled in front of them. Anyone that manages to get out of this system is deemed a threat because they will inevitably like Moses lead a rebellion against this system and bring it to a stop. Why? Because this system needs people to work! Once you get rid of people (whether on the manufacturing or more importantly the consumer end) the system comes crashing down.

He said to his people, "Look, the people of Israel now outnumber us and are stronger than we are. We must make a plan to keep them from growing even more. If we don't, and if war breaks out, they will join our enemies and fight against us. Then they will escape from the country."
Exodus 1:10-11 (NLT)

- Your job is a distraction from your work! It is because satan is too threatened by your strength and what you can produce that he will buy your talent and put you to work for chump change.

He exploited our people and oppressed our fathers, forcing them to abandon their infants so they would die.
Acts 7:19 (BSB)

- There is a nourishment that comes from doing your work that you can never get from doing a job!

"My food," said Jesus, "is to do the will of him who sent me and to finish his work.
John 4:34 (NIV)

- Make a decision today! Not to quit your job but to work yourself out of your job! When you pray you are working, when you fast, when you write your vision down all these things are working. Commit yourself to your work and believe God to establish it! Don't think of how unhappy your job makes you, set your mind on how happy your work makes you. Begin to see life rewarding you and paying you for your work! Pray this short pray below and insert your name there!

May the favour of the Lord our God rest on_____; establish the work of (MY) hands for (ME)— yes, establish the work of (MY) hands.
Psalm 90:17 (NIV)

In Jesus name!

Amen.

KOSMOS THINKERS	KINGDOM THINKERS
JOB	Work
Employment	Opportunities
Consumers	Creators (authors, bloggers, inventors, manufacturers)
Lenders	Borrowers
I work for money	Money works for me
What is my next job	What is my next business
Currency	Money
Liability and debt management	Asset management
I pay my taxes	My assets pay my taxes
I work hard at my job	I work myself out of my job

Do not conform to the pattern of this world, but be transformed by the renewing of your mind. Then you will be able to test and approve what God's will is--his good, pleasing and perfect will.
Romans 12:2 (NIV)

Fill in the blank spaces with some of your old thoughts versus your renewed thoughts!

Where are you called to work?

"Everybody is a genius. But if you judge a fish by its ability to climb a tree, it will live its whole life believing that it is stupid."
- Albert Einstein

(Circle one)

1. Business?- Economy
2. Entertainment?- Creativity
3. Government?- Authority
4. Education?- Destiny
5. Media?- Publicity
6. Religion?- Spirituality
7. Family?- Identity

Power Statement- (revisit this daily)

I _____(name) am called to _____ (i.e. creativity) through

_____
_____
_____
_____ *my work begins* __/__/____
(DD/MM/YYYY)

CHAPTER 9l MONEY VERSUS MAMMON

Give to Caesar what belongs to Caesar!

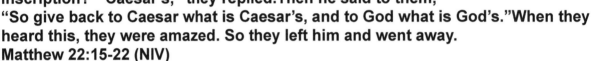

**Then the Pharisees went out and laid plans to trap him in his words. They sent their disciples to him along with the Herodians. "Teacher," they said, "we know that you are a man of integrity and that you teach the way of God in accordance with the truth. You aren't swayed by others, because you pay no attention to who they are. Tell us then, what is your opinion? Is it right to pay the imperial tax Tell us then, what is your opinion? Is it right to pay the imperial tax to Caesar or not?" But Jesus, knowing their evil intent, said, "You hypocrites, why are you trying to trap me? Show me the coin used for paying the tax." They brought him a denarius, and he asked them, "Whose image is this? And whose inscription?" "Caesar's," they replied. Then he said to them, "So give back to Caesar what is Caesar's, and to God what is God's." When they heard this, they were amazed. So they left him and went away.
Matthew 22:15-22 (NIV)**

- The Denarius was originally in 211 BC a silver minted coin. Derived from the Latin dēnī which means containing 10 because one denarius was worth ten asses. Over time this currency became debased by mixing it with other metals (a form of quantitive easing) so that one Denari bought sixteen asses as debasing it lowered its buying power.

- This is what Jesus meant by give to Caesar what belongs to Caesar and to God what belongs to God. God has money and the system of the world (cosmos) has a form of money. I say a form of money because the worlds money is ruled by satan and therefore backed by literally nothing. The Bible calls this money mammon or unrighteous mammon. Today it is more formally known as *fiat money*.

Fiat Money & What Satan does not want you to know?

Fiat money is **currency** that a government has declared to be legal tender, but it is not backed by a physical commodity. The value of **fiat money** is derived from the relationship between supply and demand rather than the value of the material that the **money** is made of.[7]

- In Satan's economy we are all playing monopoly. In this game of monopoly we are exchanging the time we should be spending on our God, children, business, husband,

---

[7] www.investopedia.com

wife, dreams and purpose for paper. This paper just like monopoly money has a value on it. The value is 10 or 50- the currency is only valuable because a government says it is valuable.

- The question by now we all need to be asking ourselves is what happens to us, our houses, our children education, our jobs when a government no longer deems its paper promises as valuable? This is what Egypt meant by

We must make a plan to keep them from growing even more.
Exodus 1:10 (NLT)

- Satan's economic structure is Egypt. The Jewish word for Egypt is *mitsrayim,* it means to limit or to siege.

- Your dream is presently being inserted into a rigged system that empowers the greedy, the rich and the evil by using the poor and working class.

- This is how a minority of wicked people own the wealth of the world. Fiat currency is not money- it is a legal government scam belonging to Caesar. This is what satan does not want you to know.

- Nations like Greece have had their citizens robbed of their savings in a day because the government decided that this form of currency was no longer valuable. When we realise that all we are working for is paper with numbers and a sovereigns face on it then we will begin a journey of wealth that the enemy will be afraid of.

Why You can't serve both God and Mammon

- Fiat currency in itself is evil because it has zero accountability to anything but greed otherwise known to the church as mammon or satan. This does not mean that we are not supposed to use it.

And I say unto you, Make to yourselves friends of the mammon of unrighteousness; that, when ye fail, they may receive you into everlasting habitations.
Luke 16:9 (KJV)

- The world by and large has grown so accustomed to fiat currency that it really has become a demonstration of their faith in the government. All the government needs to do to give currency value is raise taxes from us. Our willingness to accept paper or electronic money is truly an expression of our faith. The key to the survival of this form of currency is based on our faith and belief that it is in actual fact 'real money.'

- This is why you can't serve both God and mammon because to truly serve God requires the same faith that you are putting in the fake currency. This faith is the only thing that pleases God and when it comes to His children, He will have no rivals for it.

(Never worship any other god, because the LORD is a God who does not tolerate rivals. In fact, he is known for not tolerating rivals.)
Exodus 34:14 (GWT)

- This is why Pharaoh in the Bible did not want the children of Israel to leave Egypt. Leaving would diminish the system that he had built to siege them in. Pharaoh had established an employment strategy that would make great people live small and narrow lives from pay cheque to pay cheque and bill to bill. Mammon was his name and he was then and is now a god to many Christian believers.

- If you don't believe me, try and not show up for work tomorrow! This is what Jesus asked somebody to do who thought he was perfect.

Just then a man came up to Jesus and asked, "Teacher, what good thing must I do to get eternal life?" "Why do you ask me about what is good?" Jesus replied. "There is only One who is good. If you want to enter life, keep the commandments." "Which ones?" he inquired. Jesus replied, "'You shall not murder, you shall not commit adultery, you shall not steal, you shall not give false testimony, honour your father and mother,' and 'love your neighbour as yourself.'" "All these I have kept," the young man said. "What do I still lack?"

Jesus answered, "If you want to be perfect, go, sell your possessions and give to the poor, and you will have treasure in heaven. Then come, follow me." When the young man heard this, he went away sad, because he had great wealth. Then Jesus said to his disciples, "Truly I tell you, it is hard for someone who is rich to enter the kingdom of heaven. Again I tell you, it is easier for a camel to go through the eye of a needle than for someone who is rich to enter the kingdom of God." When the disciples heard this, they were greatly astonished and asked, "Who then can be saved?" Jesus looked at them and said, "With man this is impossible, but with God all things are possible."
Matthew 19: 16-26 (NIV)

- This man lacked the ability to let go of the faith connection to mammon to attach it to his faith connection to God. Faith makes him pleasing to God and his faith was in unrighteous mammon.

And without faith it is impossible to please God, because anyone who comes to him must believe that he exists and that he rewards those who earnestly seek him.
Hebrews 11:6 (NIV)

Inflation Simplified

Brian borrowed £10,000 from Sue. He used it to purchase 1000 cows. Brian knew he could never repay Sue the £10,000. Since he could not afford it, Brian decided that he would print it. He went to a printer and printed £10,000 (known as quantitive easing at literally little to no cost or interest charges (an advantage known as 'seignorage' by economists.) Brian knew the £10,000 had no value- nobody worked for it so he told all his children that from now on one chocolate bar from daddy would no longer cost you £1 it would now cost you £100. He did this so that he could justify the £10,000 he had just printed. Treating his own people unfairly to pay back his debt and not feel guilty about the amount of money backed by zero demand/supply was the only way to alleviate his guilt and restore the value of the integrity of £10,000. By redefining what money was and what it could buy Brian slept easier even though his children did not. This is the never ending story of inflation. Brian has started a wealth transfer from his young, vulnerable children to himself and feels little to no guilt about it. This is what the banks and our government does every day.

- Inflation is not natural, it is man made and the height of demonic evil. It is the promises politicians make to build new schools, safer public transport etc and then borrow that money from private investors and diminish our spending power so that we can pay it all back.

- This Ponzi scheme only succeeds on the faith of the people that it is in actual fact not a never ending scam.

A Brief History of Fiat Currency[8]

""The farther back you can look, the farther forward you are likely to see.""
- Sir Winston Churchill

- the Fiat currency experiment has never succeeded since its inception in the Roman empire. The adoption of fake money (mammon) ended in not only the devaluing of the Roman currency but of the economy that initiated it.

Rome

- Rome had no paper money but it had its own form of quantitative easing. Instead of printing money it debased money. By AD 54 Emperor Nero took the then pure silver denarius and made it 94% silver. By around AD 100 the denarius was now 85% silver. This mixing of silver with less precious metals is similar to what you might see in a 2 pence coin. It has little to no true value. Like printing money, debasing currency helped governments pay back bills. They could simply shave off silver from their coin and mix the remainder with a cheap lookalike but this also diminished the buying power of the Citizens of the empire. A form of wealth transfer from people to governments. By 218 the denarius was now 43% silver and by 244 the Arabic emperor Philip had the denarius down to 0.02% silver. By this time the silver coin was no longer deemed a medium of exchange or a store of value.

China

- When the Chinese started using paper money it was called 'flying money' because it could literally just fly from your hands. Paper money became a norm in china because the shortage in copper led to the use of iron which later became heavily underpriced.

- During the 11th Century China used paper money to buy iron. Paper money was then backed by gold so it was a form of receipt. China then went into war with the Mongols and lost to Genghis Khan. His grandson Kublai Khan united China and assumed

---

[8] https://dailyreckoning.com/fiat-currency/

emperorship. Kublai succeeded with fiat currency after running into issues with paper money backed by gold. Marco Polo said of him:

"You might say that [Kublai] has the secret of alchemy in perfection…the Khan causes every year to be made such a vast quantity of this money, which costs him nothing, that it must equal in amount all the treasure of the world."

- Marco Polo then went on to conclude:

"Population and trade had greatly increased, but the emissions of paper notes were suffered to largely outrun both…All the beneficial effects of a currency that is allowed to expand with a growth of population and trade were now turned into those evil effects that flow from a currency emitted in excess of such growth. These effects were not slow to develop themselves…The best families in the empire were ruined, a new set of men came into the control of public affairs, and the country

became the scene of internecine warfare and confusion."

France

- The death of Louis XIV and the 3 billion lives of debt he left behind greatly helped the notion of paper money.

- When Louis XV under the advisement of John Law (first brought paper money to France) became of age he demanded that all debts be paid in paper money backed by coinage. The problem started when people no longer content with their paper promises started to demand their coins as the paper promises became massively oversupplied.

- The system collapsed after failed attempts of the citizens to exchange their paper promises for cash and John Law became the most hated man in all of France and fled to Italy.

- France tried again with its paper promises experiment in the 18th Century. The paper money was now called assignats. By 1975 the assignats inflation was 13,000%. Napoleon rescued France by bringing in the gold franc. He realised that gold is the secret to a stable economy and that ensued for the duration of his reign.

- After the War of Waterloo the French gave paper money another go in the 1930's with the paper franc. It only took 12 years for the currency to inflate and lose 99% of its value.

Germany

- Post world war one Weimar Germany was one of the greatest periods of hyper inflation and the Treaty of Versailles was Germanys financial punishment to make reparations.

- The sum of reparation was too much so Germany turned to the printing press to pay its huge debts. Inflation got so bad that German citizens were using stacks of marks (German paper money) to heat their furnaces as their paper promises amounted to nothing.

April 1919: 1US dollar=12 marks
November 1921: 1US dollar= 263 marks
January 1923: 1US dollar= 17,000 marks
August 1923: 1US dollar= 4.621 million marks
October 1923: 1US dollar= 25.26 billion marks
December 1923: 1US dollar= 4.2 trillion marks.

More Recent: Argentina, Mexico, Thai baht, Russia Zimbabwe

In 1932, Argentina had the eighth largest economy in the world before its currency collapsed. In 1992, Finland, Italy, and Norway had currency shocks that spread through Europe.

In 1994, Mexico went through the infamous "Tequila Hangover," which sent the peso tumbling and spread economic hardships throughout Latin America.
In 1997, the Thai baht fell through the floor and the effects spread to Malaysia, the Philippines, Indonesia, Hong Kong, and South Korea.

The Russian ruble was not the currency you wanted your investments denominated in in 1998, after its devaluation brought on economic recession. In the early 21st century, we have seen the Turkish lira experience strokes of hyperinflation similar to that of the mark of Weimar Germany.

In present times, we have Zimbabwe, which was once considered the breadbasket of Africa and was one of the wealthiest countries on the continent. Now Mugabe's attempts at price controls, combined with hyperinflation, have the nation unable to supply the most basic essentials such as bread and clean water.

The Only way satan's system can work!

- There is only one way satan's system can work. is if the currency in question is accountable to a commodity. Such a commodity would need to have lasting life as a store of value so that £1 will always equal that amounts store of value.

- It is not enough to say it is backed by a commodity it must indeed be backed by the commodity.

- Mammon is a greedy, evil spirit that perverts money, turning it into paper promises backed by lies.

- The only way currency can work is if it is backed by money (which belongs to God) and lets face it, the devil is not going to allow that to happen any time soon. Well at least until his system fails again.

- Every time the system has crashed Nations have always:
  1. Borrowed money.
  2. Raised taxes on the middle and working class.
  3. Quantitative easing- printed money to cover greed, war, corruption and debt.
  4. Reverted back to a commodity of accountability (real money) to rescue themselves from certain failure.

What is Money?

Now that we know that money is not currency and that money is not evil but currency is, let's look at what money actually is. God delights in you having money and lots of it!

**LET THEM SHOUT FOR JOY, AND BE GLAD, THAT FAVOUR MY RIGHTEOUS CAUSE: YEA, LET THEM SAY CONTINUALLY, LET THE LORD BE MAGNIFIED, WHICH HATH PLEASURE IN THE PROSPERITY OF HIS SERVANT.
PSALM 35:27 (KJV)**

Find a table on the difference between currency and money on the next page.[9]

CURRENCY	MONEY
A medium of exchange	A medium of exchange
A unit of account (has numbers on it)	A unit of account
Portable	Portable
Durable	Durable- Does not corrode
Divisible (make change)	Divisible- Make change
Fungible (inexchangable- each unit is the same as the same unit with someone else).	Fungible (inexchangable- each unit is the same as the next unit).
Is not a store of value (due to quantitive easing- governments ability to print it).	A store of value over a long period of time (limited in quantity, governments cannot print it)

- The difference between money and currency is money is a store of value over a long period of time because it is limited in quantity and governments cannot print it.

- When we realise that no fiat currency in human history has ever survived- the future of our paper pound notes or US dollar notes looks pretty grim.

Mike Maloney- Hidden Secrets of money

The only difference between the £5 monopoly currency and the £5 British Note below is that the Government says the £5 note is legal tender. The moment a government wishes that the £5 is too expensive to pay back its debts it will cheapen it to pay off its debts. By diminishing your spend power, governments perform legal bank robbery and reduce your currency to monopoly to pay their deficits.

If you take a close look at your own paper currency you start to see a promissory note left by the treasurer of the bank of England. It reads:

"I promise to pay the bearer on demand the sum of"

This promise now redundant made this now paper currency a type of receipt for depositing a commodity with the bank. Carrying expensive commodities was risky and heavy. You could not put diamonds in your wallet so you deposited them in banks in exchange for paper promises which upon request you could return your promise note in exchange for your commodity. This is why this signage is pasted on the top of every British Pound and every US dollar. We can all agree that the value is the commodity not the receipt.

Money Belongs to God!

- Currencies do not store your economic energy but money does! Currency leaks it through taxes, inflation, quantitative easing. Money stores it through constantly increasing and decreasing in value across time. Money answers to supply/demand currency answers to whoever is in government at the time and how much of it they want to print.

- Did you know God owns money- not mammon! Money belongs to God.

**The silver is mine and the gold is mine,' declares the LORD Almighty.
Haggai 2:8 (NIV)**

- Money is God's unit of exchange and this is what Jesus means by:

**"Then give back to Caesar what is Caesar's, and to God what is God's."
Luke 20:25 (NIV)**

- The trading standard of the world is the dollar. The US experienced decades of success that landed them the strap line 'The American Dream' because they had free markets and their dollar was backed by gold. It wasn't until Richard Nixon came in August 1971 and took the dollar off the gold standard putting the global economy under the demise of an unaccountable promissory note that the ideal of the American dream started to wither away under the weight of trillions of dollars in debt.

- Gold is only formed when a star explodes (a supernova) and it stays around for thousands of years. This is what makes it the ultimate money. (God's money!)

- It's divisible, permanent, a unit of account, it doesn't go away and it can't be increased! It keeps government under control. It will restrain governments from spending beyond their means because they can't print gold.

Inflation[10]= An expansion of the currency supply- (eventually prices rise)
Deflation= Is a contraction on the currency supply- (eventually prices fall)

- Prices aren't necessarily going up the value of the currency is going down!

- Gold and silver does not go through inflation or deflation just high value low value mediums.

---

[10] Milton Friedman. American economist July 31, 1912 – November 16, 2006

How Wealth Transfer will happen

A good person leaves an inheritance for their children's children, but a sinner's wealth is stored up for the righteous.
Proverbs 13:22 (NIV)

- The most significant example of this can be found in the Book of Exodus where an economy was built surrounding a people the enemy did not want to know were great.

He said to his people, "Look, the people of Israel now outnumber us and are stronger than we are.
Exodus 1:9 (NLT)

- In this system:

1. Israel were given tough and strenuous jobs with brutal socialist employees that made them work extra hard for little to no pay.

Therefore they set taskmasters over them to afflict them with heavy burdens.
Exodus 1:11 (ESV)

2. They had a banking system to control currency and keep money in the hands of the rich and out of the hands of the working class. A system entirely rigged to favour the rich.

They built for Pharaoh store cities, Pithom and Raamses.
Exodus 1:11 (ESV)

3. There was an attempt to control wealth and resources by controlling the size of the population.

THE KING OF EGYPT SAID TO THE HEBREW MIDWIVES, WHOSE NAMES WERE SHIPHRAH AND PUAH, "WHEN YOU ARE HELPING THE HEBREW WOMEN DURING CHILDBIRTH ON THE DELIVERY STOOL, IF YOU SEE THAT THE BABY IS A BOY, KILL HIM; BUT IF IT IS A GIRL, LET HER LIVE."
EXODUS 1:15-16 (NIV)

- In the midst of an extremely controlling climate, God had a saviour in the form of Moses. A man to whom He would send on this assignment:

He said, "But I will be with you, and this shall be the sign for you, that I have sent you: when you have brought the people out of Egypt, you shall serve God on this mountain."
Exodus 3:12 (ESV)

- It would seem as though God was setting them free from a job to give them another job. God was setting them free from a job to give them their work! Their jobs fed their stomach but their work feeds their soul.

- God releases his strategy for destroying Egypt (Limitation in Hebrew):

And I will give this people favour in the sight of the Egyptians; and when you go, you shall not go empty, but each woman shall ask of her neighbour, and any woman who lives in her house, for silver and gold jewellery, and for clothing. You shall put them on your sons and on your daughters. So you shall plunder the Egyptians."
Exodus 3:21-22 (NIV)

- The church will yet again see a great wealth transfer as God reclaims what is rightfully His from the wicked and clothes His church with it.

and he that is feeble among them at that day shall be as David; and the house of David shall be as God, as the angel of the LORD before them.
Zechariah 12:8 (KJV)

CHAPTER 10l TAKING BACK WORLD KINGDOMS

Taking Back World Kingdoms

The seventh angel sounded his trumpet, and there were loud voices in heaven, which said: "The kingdom of the world has become the kingdom of our Lord and of his Messiah, and he will reign for ever and ever."
Revelation 11:15

- The final trumpet is going to sound, signalling that the Kingdom of this world have become the Kingdom of our God and of His Christ. We get to be a part of that final trumpet call before the coming of the Lord.

- Now that you have been equipped with kingdom truths it is now time to discover practical ways for you to engage world systems and bring them back to God.

- The Bible tells us that satan is the god of this world. A word that we have already discussed that means
  1. World order
  2. World systems
  3. World currency
  4.. Worldly people

- When the Bible says in John 3:16 that God so loved the world and then John says in 1 John 2:15 do not love the world or anything in the world, these two statements can appear in stark contrast with one another.

- When we understand it from a Kingdom perspective it can easily be understood as God loving the people trapped in satan's sinister world order and that we are instructed not to love the world system that they are trapped in but to effectively hate it enough to want to alter it forever so that people can be saved through bold, faith-filled Christians heaven bent on dramatically changing it forever!

- These believers will love people and use currency, systems and world orders. They will not love systems, currency, world orders and use people!

- The goal here is that you have to see yourself as a new breed of missionary. You are no longer prescribing to the late Billy Graham's powerful mantra of - *winning the lost one soul at a time!* Although powerful in its day! You are now moving into a new dispensation- a 7th trumpet blast which causes you to operate on a basis where you are winning lost systems many souls at a time!

- How do you take back world systems?

1. Know your Sphere of authority!

To truly take back world systems you must develop a prayer life consistent with the sphere of operation that Christ has called you to! Many Christians find prayer boring because they do not understand that our sphere or realm of authority in prayer must always be consistent with the domain that God has prescribed to us whether

1. Geographically- Location
2. Demographically- age, status, social class
3. Psychographically- behavioural, archetypes
4. Systemically- Business, Government, Media, Entertainment, Family, Education, Religion.

Before you say 'let your kingdom come!' You must know where you intend His Kingdom to come to! This means that you must have a thorough understanding of the aforementioned domains. Audacity is nothing less than ignorant authority! When you don't know what God has made you an authority over then your prayers are less effective than partnering with somebody who is an authority in that area. The truth is, there are places, systems and people God will forbid you to touch! Not because they are evil but because they are beyond your purview!

And they went through the region of Phrygia and Galatia, having been forbidden by the Holy Spirit to speak the word in Asia.
Acts 16:6

You would think that go into all the world and preach literally meant go everywhere and anywhere but it was an instruction to a people who understood their demographic!

These twelve Jesus sent out with the following instructions: "Do not go among the Gentiles or enter any town of the Samaritans. Go rather to the lost sheep of Israel.
Matthew 10:5-6

Even Jesus never went beyond Jewish boundaries because it was a space reserved for Apostle Paul! Jesus understood where He was called to bring God's Kingdom to!

He answered, "I was sent only to the lost sheep of Israel."
Matthew 15:24

Jesus only went to Gentile (non Jewish) territory once and this is what happened when He tried to cast out a demon there!

And they cried out, saying, "What business do we have with each other, Son of God? Have You come here to torment us before the time?"
Matthew 8:29

The demons cried out- What Business do we have with each other! These demons could negotiate with Jesus because although He had power to cast them out He was in Gentile territory where He had no authority to drive them out! These demons never left the City, they went into some pigs not because Jesus was being merciful but He had no permission to reach them as they were not His demographic! Those demons knew their rights!

This is what James meant by:

You do not have, because you do not ask. You ask and do not receive, because you ask wrongly
James 4:2-3

What if we are asking wrongly because we are trying to go into a measure, field, job, business, ministry that does not belong to us! Paul said there is nothing wrong with boasting as long as you are boasting about something that God has given to you to do that you are excellent at! When boasting goes from confidence to arrogance it is because you are exerting undue influence in an area that you have no authority in.

We do not dare to classify or compare ourselves with some who commend themselves. When they measure themselves by themselves and compare themselves with themselves, they are not wise. We, however, will not boast beyond proper limits, but will confine our boasting to the sphere of service God himself has assigned to us, a sphere that also includes you.
2 Corinthians 10:12-13

What is the sphere God has called you to and what part within that sphere are you called to fulfil? (business, media, government, education, family, entertainment, religion)

_____
_____
_____

What Country or City has God called you to?

_____
_____
_____

2. Know your End

When God speaks to us prophetically, He always speaks of the end! Whether it is a dream or a vision, God is calling our attention to the end part of the story.

I am God, and there is no other; I am God, and there is none like me. I make known the end from the beginning, from ancient times, what is still to come. I say, 'My purpose will stand, and I will do all that I please.'
Isaiah 46:9-10

God will show you through dreams, visions and prophets the end from the beginning! Then He will encourage you at a time where your situation and your revelation don't align with this prophetic message!

For I know the thoughts that I think toward you, saith the LORD, thoughts of peace, and not of evil, to give you an expected end.
Jeremiah 29:11

God tells us that evil is just a part of the story line to the end picture that He showed you! God shows Joseph a dream in Genesis 37. The dream was an end product of God's plan for his life and His entire generation. According to Isaiah 46 God is not revealing our purpose, God is revealing His purpose and our part to play in His purpose. That is all vision really is! When vision becomes 'mine' it is no longer vision but ambition!

Get a list of your dreams and visions, write them down and interpret them with other prophetic people and you will see that all God is showing you is the end and final destination of your part in His purpose.

And the LORD answered me: "Write the vision; make it plain on tablets, so he may run who reads it. This vision is for a future time. It describes the end, and it will be fulfilled. If it seems slow in coming, wait patiently, for it will surely take place. It will not be delayed.
Habakkuk 2:2-3

Every dream and vision is a parable describing the end picture of God's Kingdom plan for your life waiting for you to make it plain by interpretation so that you can walk in the fulness of its instruction.

It is the glory of God to conceal a matter; to search out a matter is the glory of kings.
Proverbs 25:2

When God makes manifest dreams and visions, He holds instructions within them that if followed can unlock immense kingdom fortune!

For God does speak--now one way, now another-- though no one perceives it. In a dream, in a vision of the night, when deep sleep falls on people as they slumber in their beds, Then He opens the ears of men, And seals their instruction,
Job 33:14-15

Ask God to give you a vision or a dream of His end purpose for your life? Write it down below!

Now prayerfully ask God for an interpretation using the Bible to help you understand the symbols or seek those out who are anointed for this!

_____
_____
_____
_____
_____
_____
_____
_____
_____
_____
_____

Ask God What are the Instructions within the dream?

_____
_____
_____
_____
_____
_____
_____
_____
_____
_____
_____

3. Understand the 'whatever' anointing!

The most frustrated people in Christianity are people who know what God has called them to do, More so frustrated than people who don't because there is a sense of deep sorrow with why where they are is not aligning with what God said about that final end picture. God points this out often in scripture describing the end as something magnificent but the beginning as always being something small.

**Though thy beginning was small, yet thy latter end should greatly increase.
Job 8:7**

**The end of a matter is better than its beginning, and patience is better than pride.
Ecclesiastes 7:8**

The truth is, we all have to start small.

Might it be that where you think you ought to end is hindering you from where you ought to begin?

Joseph knew he was called to greatness. He spoke about it often to his brothers who hated him for sharing his dreams. His greatness journey began with cleaning toilets for a man called Potiphar. He went from toilet cleaner to Prime Minister of a Nation.

Nehemiah knew he was a mighty builder, he started his journey as a butler for a government building.

People ask me all the time, how do I start? You start by getting yourself within the gates of the sphere you are called to by any means necessary. I call this the 'whatever anointing!'

**Once these signs are fulfilled, do whatever your hand finds to do, for God is with you.
1 Samuel 10:7**

Once you start seeing the horizon of your dream and vision beginning to manifest then you position yourself within the sphere and location of your destiny and do there whatever your hands find to do! It is from that place of doing whatever somewhere specific that God who is with you will promote you!

You cannot do 'whatever' wherever! You must do it somewhere specific to what God told you! In essence if God told you that you were going to be a news anchor for the BBC, then you should be by the 'whatever' anointing applying for the 'whatever' job within that place knowing that God is with you and if he can take Joseph a toilet cleaner and make him a prime minister then he can take you a receptionist and make you a news anchor! The 'whatever' anointing only works with right positioning. Once you understand with specificity the location God wants you to be in then you can do whatever when you get there and as long as you do it with all your heart then God will be with you and promote you. You cannot do whatever, wherever, however! You must do whatever, somewhere and with the same standard of excellence that you would apply when the spot light is on you!

**Whatever you find to do with your hands, do it with all your might,
Ecclesiastes 9:10**

Whatever you do, work at it with your whole being, for the Lord and not for men, Colossians 3:23

When Joseph was cleaning toilets as a slave he was the most successful slave in Potiphar's house!

**And the LORD was with Joseph, and he was a prosperous man; and he was in the house of his master the Egyptian.
Genesis 39:2**

When Joseph was a prisoner accused of rape he applied the 'whatever' anointing and it worked there too!

**The warden paid no attention to anything under Joseph's care, because the LORD was with Joseph and gave him success in whatever he did.
Genesis 39:23**

Joseph was the most well behaved, most excellent and most prosperous prisoner there was because as long as he was within the vicinity of God's promised greatness Joseph always knew that he was just one step, one person and one more shift away from the palace.

Are you willing to start small?

_____

Which Place are you called to: (Hollywood, Sony Records, Harvard Teacher,)

_____

What job, opportunity, apprenticeship are you going to apply for within the vicinity of where God promised your greatness? (The Whatever anointing)

_____
_____
_____
_____
_____
_____
_____
_____
_____
_____

Which friends already within your sphere are you going to associate with this year?

_____
_____
_____
_____
_____
_____
_____
_____
_____
_____
_____
_____
_____

Thank you for reading 'Kingdom Secrets.' It is our hope that you use this guide as a tool to train others with what you have heard. Please kindly help us by becoming a fan and leaving a review on our Facebook page: Find us on Facebook by searching:

'millionaire maker project.'

Send us pictures of your project groups and testimonies of how the book is helping change lives on your social media by hash tagging

#kingdomsecrets

on twitter, Instagram or Facebook. Continue Kingdom SecretsJourney with us on our Facebook page and receive access to live webinars and videos resources.

CPSIA information can be obtained
at www.ICGtesting.com
Printed in the USA
BVHW010308131121
621491BV00005B/285